Puppy Training, a Smart Owner's Guide®
part of the Kennel Club Books® Interactive Series®
ISBN: 978-1-593787-86-8 ©2010

Kennel Club Books Inc., 40 Broad St., Freehold, NJ 07728. Printed in China.
All rights reserved. No part of this book may be reproduced in any form, by Photostat, scanner, microfilm, xerography or any other means, or incorporated into any information retrieval system, electronic or mechanical, without the written permission of the copyright owner.

photographers include Isabelle Francias/BowTie Inc.;
Gina Cioli and Pamela Hunnicutt/BowTie Inc.

For CIP information, see page 176.

P9-DOA-004

K9 EXPERT

Congratulations! You are about to bring a new puppy into your home and are committed to training him to be the best dog he can be. That is just the kind of enthusiasm we like to see in a new owner.

Are you wondering when to start training? The correct answer is: The minute you bring him home. Years ago, trainers believed you needed to wait until a puppy was 6 months old before he could retain any training information. Happily, times (and peoples' views) have changed. Good breeders start handling their puppies as soon as they're born so that the pups become accustomed to human touch. Even before their eyes and ears open, puppies are held, their nails are clipped and they are gently combed, introducing them to the sensations and routines that will become part of their lives forever.

As the puppies' eyes open, they grow more adventurous and begin to explore their environments. Breeders expose them to new stimuli: a variety of flooring and footing; the noise of the dishwasher, the vacuum cleaner and the TV; and the activity of a busy household. Many breeders put a crate into the puppies' play area, to make the pups completely comfortable while they rest and sleep in their little dens.

One of the advantages of getting your puppy from a knowledgeable breeder is that a lot of good habits have already been

PUPPY TRAINING

by Miriam Fields–Babineau and Bardi McLennan

SMART OWNER'S GUIDE™

FROM THE EDITORS OF DOGFANCY. MAGAZINE

CONTENTS

established. The puppy has slept in a crate, has had his nails trimmed weekly, has had a few baths and is accustomed to human handling. Continue these good habits, and you'll be off to a great start. Stop reinforcing these habits for just a week, and your puppy will forget everything his breeder taught him and become an unmannered nuisance. That may be cute for a day but not for much longer. Razor-sharp puppy teeth hurt!

It's important that you puppy-proof the room your puppy will be staying in. The kitchen is a popular choice because it is usually where everyone congregates and the floor can handle accidents. Fill his crate with some safe toys and a cozy blanket that has the scent of his mother and littermates on it, and encourage him to nap inside by using treats. Block open doorways with baby gates and secure loose cupboards with bungee cords. Take your puppy out immediately on leash after meals and naps, returning to the same spot and encouraging him to eliminate by using the same word. At night, bring the crate into your bedroom but resist the urge to let him sleep with you. If you allow it the first night, he will sleep with you forever.

Once he's had his vaccinations, enroll him in a puppy kindergarten class. These sessions may benefit you even more than your puppy. They allow him to socialize with other dogs but also teach him that he must follow your cues despite the distractions. The classes will teach you the right tone of voice to use — gentle but firm — and the appropriate hand signals to reinforce your verbal cues.

Once your puppy is well trained, he'll be a joy to live with. He will be welcomed in

JOIN OUR ONLINE Club Pup™

With this Smart Owner's Guide™, you are well on your way to getting your puppy-training diploma. But your puppy education doesn't end here.

You're invited to join **Club Pup™ (DogChannel.com/Club-Pup)**, a FREE online site with lots of fun and instructive features such as:

◆ **forums, blogs** and **profiles** where you can connect with other puppy owners
◆ **downloadable charts** and **checklists** to help you be a smart and loving puppy owner
◆ interactive **games**
◆ canine **quizzes**

The **Smart Owner's Guide** series and **Club Pup** are backed by the experts at DOG FANCY® magazine and DogChannel.com — who have been providing trusted and up-to-date information about dogs and dog people for more than 40 years. Log on and join the club today!

your community and will make you proud whether you're travelling with him, entertaining guests at home or just hanging out with the family. Understand that he wants to please you, but he needs consistency and clear instruction to be able to do it.

Allan Reznik
Editor-at-Large, DOG FANCY

CHAPTER 1

SETTING THE

STAGE

When pups are about 3 weeks old and just beginning to wobble about and venture from their mothers, they instinctively walk away from their sleeping areas to relieve themselves. You might say that pups are naturally housetrained.

So when you bring your puppy home for the first time, you'll need to take over where Mother Nature leaves off. Your first step in housetraining will be to teach your puppy to relieve himself only in approved areas. Then, your duties will consist of teaching your pup the acceptable doggie behavior in and around your house: what areas are off limits, how to react to strangers at the door, how to interact with young children, etc.

To achieve your housetraining goals, you must be rigidly consistent, alert and patient because even when your puppy's bladder has matured enough to "hold it" a little longer between potty trips, you must not think of him as housetrained. Your pup still has a lot more to learn.

There are several approaches to the initial phase of housetraining. Stick with whichever method you choose, so that your pup won't get confused and you won't become frustrated. Remember, too, that success de-

> **Did You Know?** Cleaning accidents properly with an enzyme solution will dramatically reduce the time it takes to housetrain your puppy because she won't be drawn back as easily to the same locations.

pends not only on the age of your puppy but also on your level of experience with dogs, the type of home in which you live (apartment, condo, single-family house, etc.), the layout of your home (multilevel or single floor), your daily routine, your work schedule and the other members of your family.

In simple terms, housetraining comes down to getting your puppy to the right place at the right time.

TIME AND SPACE

Your puppy's age and where he came from will determine how quickly and easily he can be housetrained. Three-week-old pups instinctively want to keep their sleeping areas clean, but those instincts are stifled when humans step into the picture to prepare the pups to live with people.

An 8- to 10-week-old puppy from a responsible breeder, for example, may have had some initial cratetraining or exposure to a crate. He probably will be familiar with an exercise pen, as well, which he shared with his littermates.

Puppies of the same age that come from pet stores or shelters, however, are often more difficult to housetrain. It's not because the pups are less intelligent. It's simply because no one started training them, and

they have had to relieve themselves wherever they happen to be. In pet stores, that means soiling their crates, which makes cratetraining at home more difficult. In shelters, there are generally far fewer very young puppies, and therefore older pups and dogs are usually kept in kennel stalls with concrete floors. The older ones may have the advantage of being taken for walks by volunteers several times a day, but that's physical exercise, not housetraining. Neither group of animals can be expected to understand our ideas of cleanliness. Even though they can definitely be housetrained (barring the existence of a medical problem), it's easy to understand why it will take longer and require a lot more patience.

Where you get your puppy will also determine how much information you have about him. You know that a pup from a responsible breeder has been at the breeder's kennel since birth. A pup (or an older dog) from a shelter usually comes to you with little or no information about his

it's a **Fact**

Ongoing housetraining difficulties may indicate your puppy has a health problem, warranting a veterinary checkup. A urinary infection, parasites, a virus or other nasty issues can greatly affect a puppy's ability to hold her pee or poop.

previous life, partly depending on whether he was relinquished by his previous owners or picked up as a stray.

Dogs end up in shelters for countless reasons; not all shelter dogs were neglected or mistreated. Shelter-dog owners shouldn't use that as an excuse for their dogs' misbehavior or difficulty in training. They just need a positive outlook to get their pets going in the right direction. Regardless of a

shelter dog's actual age, begin housetraining an older dog as you would an 8- to 10-week-old puppy, until you and the dog are better acquainted and can begin to understand each other. It may take more time and more patience on your part.

RESCUE RESOURCES

Most breed clubs have their own rescue programs, whereby knowledgeable breed

SMART TIP!

If you don't live close enough to go home during your lunch breaks or if you need to work overtime, make alternative arrangements for letting your pup take her potty breaks. Hire a pet sitter, contact a pet-walking service or enlist the aid of an obliging neighbor.

experts put adoptable dogs through an evaluation process to ensure that each dog goes to the best home. Finding the right adoption fit early on hopefully reduces the likelihood of the dog returning through a "rescue revolving door." When they are picked up for rescue, these dogs are first checked by a veterinarian and spayed or neutered thereafter (or before being adopted, at the latest).

Most breed-rescue groups arrange for new dogs to live in foster homes for a while before they are adopted out, so that a

Before adopting them out, most breed rescue groups foster incoming dogs, to discern their temperaments.

knowledgeable person can evaluate the nature and extent of previous training (if any); the dog's temperament; his reactions to other dogs, cats and kids; and the dog's housetraining status.

Groups that rescue dogs of all breeds and mixed breeds also perform general evaluations. Even if little is known about the dogs when they are taken in, these rescue volunteers and foster families try to learn all they possibly can about the dogs while readying them for adoption, so that they can inform potential owners of their findings.

FEAR FACTOR

Beware of the fear phase, which affects older puppies between 4 and 6 months of age. During this time, puppies shy away from or seem to be frightened by perfectly normal sights or sounds that they have never reacted to before. If you get a puppy of this age (or when your puppy reaches this stage), do not coddle or try to soothe him. Never pick him up to cuddle and comfort him or coo at him, saying things like, "Poor little dog, it's OK." Those actions only tell your pup that it's acceptable to be shy or frightened and that you approve of his reactions.

To minimize this fear during housetraining, find a quiet spot where your puppy can relieve himself rather than at the curbside of a bustling street. If you go about your daily routine in a normal way, though, your puppy will usually grow out of this phase quickly.

Another thing to avoid at all times — before, during and after this fear phase — is pulling back on your dog's leash when meeting friendly dogs

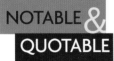

NOTABLE & QUOTABLE

It's normal for an 8-week-old puppy to pee and poop up to 20 times in 24 hours, whereas an adult dog may only go three to five times in a day.

— Denise Nord, certified pet dog trainer and owner of Canine Connection Training in Rogers, Minn.

or people. This common puppy-owner mistake will actually increase a puppy's fear or make him aggressive. He needs your upbeat voice telling him all's well in his world. He does not need protection from friendly dogs or people. In fact, the opposite is true. He needs to socialize with people and friendly dogs as much as possible. If you're not sure of the approaching dog or person, distract your puppy with cheerful chatter and walk on by. Interestingly enough, a true fear phase may last only a few days; some dogs go through it in one brief episode, while others never experience it at all.

THE OLDER DOG

If your dog is a year old or older and he has never been housetrained, you have a real job on your hands. Be prepared to put in plenty of quality time with this dog; you will need to be extremely patient and 100-percent consistent.

Don't take your eyes off your dog while training even for a minute, especially if your dog is a male. Males tend to leave a few drops after a quick, easily missed leg lift, whereas females squat and fully empty their bladders. If he lifts his leg on a piece of furniture where you don't see it, he'll go back to use the same spot even weeks later, and this could happen all over the house.

If you are trying to housetrain an older dog, one thing in your favor is that the dog's "plumbing" is mature; he can wait longer than a very young puppy can wait between potty breaks, so this part of housetraining could possibly be accomplished in a much shorter time than with his younger counterpart.

THE SEASON FOR SELECTING

For housetraining purposes, the very best time to get a puppy is when at least one family member will be home almost all day long. (However, quick shopping trips can be accomplished during predictable puppy nap times, such as after a walk or a meal.) The most difficult housetraining situation occurs when a puppy is brought into a home where everyone is at work or school during the day.

Puppies cannot housetrain themselves to their new owners' schedules! For this reason alone, it is more successful for such a family to begin with an older, housetrained dog. But if your heart is set on a puppy, wait to get him until the start of a vacation period so that at least someone, if not everyone, in the family will be home all day to start the housetraining routine and get the puppy acquainted with his new life and surroundings.

By the time your regular weekday work schedule starts again, you will have introduced your pup to his crate and his "safe" room (or exercise pen) where he will stay safely when no one is home. By getting him used to a housetraining routine and his crate (or "doggie den") while people are around, he will be more comfortable when he is left home alone.

ACCIDENTS

Let's face it, accidents will happen. No one is a perfect dog teacher, and no puppy immediately learns when and where he's "gotta go." Supervision is the key to prevention, and prevention is your key to success! If you catch your puppy in the act of eliminating where he shouldn't, you must show him your displeasure instantly but briefly. Then, if possible, move him to where he's supposed to go.

There's no need for shouting or yelling, and definitely no hitting. A single, firm "No!" or "Shame!" is enough.

How often does a puppy do her business? A lot! Go to **DogChannel. com/Club-Pup** and download the typical puppy schedule for peeing and pooping. You can also download a chart that you can fill out to track your puppy's elimination timetable, which will help you manage you pup's housetraining.

JOIN OUR
ONLINE
Club
Pup™

SMART TIP!

For maximum health and social benefits, your puppy should be spayed (female) or neutered (male) before she or he hits puberty. Studies have found that, given altered anesthesia protocols, it's safe to perform spays and neuters on puppies as young as 6 weeks old, and young pups recover faster and with less pain than older puppies.

Instead of overusing the word "No," try giving him a firm warning, such as "Aacht!" said with a scowl. It's short, sharp and seems to be as easily understood by pups as "Don't do that again" and "Don't even think about it." Never make the mistake of using your pup's name with a correction; you should only use his name to get his attention and whenever he's being a "good dog."

Take a moment to reconstruct the scenario of the accident. Was anyone keeping an eye on him? Were you paying attention when he circled or started running back and forth? When was he last taken out?

Your primary job with a puppy or a new dog of any age is to pay attention. At first, someone must watch him every moment he's awake. Don't think that your pup is housetrained just because he hasn't had an accident in 10 days. That's a great start, but if you let down your guard, unnecessary accidents will occur; you can count on it.

When an accident has happened in the house, put your puppy in his crate while you clean up the mess. You don't need the culprit as a spectator. Then use any one of the numerous products now on the market to remove both the stain and the odor.

Remember, urine or fecal odors send a strong signal to the puppy to use the same spot again. After the accident is cleaned up (and you've calmed down), have some fun playtime with your puppy so you can both get over the accident.

By now, you may have figured out why we strongly suggest that you get your puppy at a time when someone will be home all day or at the beginning of a vacation period. Housetraining is extremely difficult — not just for you, but more so for the puppy — if no one is home all day. If you are only able to take some vacation time to start housetraining when you get your dog, then you'll need to go home to let him out during your lunch breaks or find someone to help once your family's normal schedule resumes. After first taking your new pup out to relieve himself, it's best if someone can play with him for a little while, give him lunch, take him outside again to go potty. Then they should leave him clean, fed and content in his safe area until another family member returns.

Your puppy will look to you for potty rules. Be consistent and disciplined in your training.

NOTABLE & QUOTABLE

A puppy might forget what he's supposed to do outside; pups are easily distracted. It's up to the owner to make sure elimination actually happens. If [he doesn't eliminate right away], go back inside, crate the pup for five minutes or so, then take him out and try again.

— Victoria Schade, certified pet dog trainer and owner of Good Dog! Obedience Training in Annandale, Va.

PREPARATIONS

Before you bring home a new puppy, you must do some homework and preplanning. The more prepared you are, the more successful your housetraining efforts will be.

For starters, you should line up a good veterinarian. You never know when an emergency will occur, so it's good to have someone already on your speed dial. Plus, you'll want to schedule an initial visit within a couple of days of bringing your puppy home, so the veterinarian can make sure the puppy is healthy and determine baselines for future visits.

Ask for vet recommendations from friends or neighbors who own dogs, and check out any that sound promising, to see if they are taking new patients; perhaps visit a couple in order to see the facilities and meet the staff. Find out if you can stop by for a few minutes while you are bringing your puppy home for the first time. That way, he can get to know the office, be petted by the receptionist, check out the lobby and maybe even meet the vet. This visit should not include a

it's a Fact

Dogs are descendants of wolves. You can think of your puppy's crate as a modern-day den. A multipurpose crate serves as a bed, a housetraining tool and a travel carrier. It also is the ideal doggie den — a bedroom of sorts — that your puppy can retire to when she wants to rest or just needs a break.

SMART TIP!

For a few days after the initial house tour, some owners find it easier to restrain their lively, squirming puppies by attaching a very short piece of an old leash to the collar. It's easier to grab than trying to put your fingers through a collar. Just be sure it is short enough that your puppy cannot reach her mouth to chew it.

checkup or anything of that nature. It's simply so the puppy can associate the vet's office as a safe and enjoyable place, where he gets a lot of attention from happy, nice people. A few days later, you can bring him in for an "official" visit. At that time, be sure to bring all the health records that the breeder or rescue organization provided, as well as a stool sample (see page 27 for instructions on collecting samples).

THE FIRST PIT STOP

Before you even bring your new puppy home for the first time, you should have decided where his potty spot will be. Before he goes inside to meet the family, he will need to "go" outside. As soon as you arrive home, take him to the designated spot. This pit stop will help your puppy associate the appropriate place to go to the bathroom.

You must decide precisely where the pup's potty spot will be. After he's gone potty in several places on your lawn, any and all grass under his feet will tell him he's in the right spot, and it will be difficult for you to persuade him otherwise. Shelter dogs that were kept on concrete

floors will most likely prefer to relieve themselves on the pavement during a walk or on your concrete patio, such as beside your pool or garden walkways.

Start the training in the manner you intend to continue. If you have a fenced yard, here's a great idea to save the lawn, bushes, flower beds and your own sanity: Select a corner or a small area about 8- to 12-feet-long by 3-feet-wide; alongside your house or garage is ideal, especially if it is under eaves or an overhang that will keep it dry year-round. Block off the area either with secure fencing material and metal posts, or by attaching a kennel run or an exercise pen. Be sure that whatever fencing you use has a gate that can securely close.

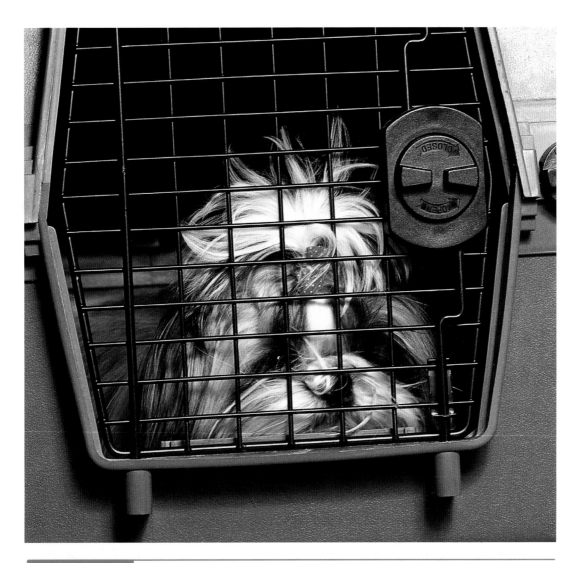

NOTABLE & QUOTABLE

A crate can save your dog's life. Dogs, especially puppies, have been known to eat disturbing things — light bulbs, golf balls, pantyhose, even small knives. If you have a puppy that is in the chewing stage, keep him confined in a crate to prevent him from eating something that can harm him. Leaving a puppy loose in a house where he can chew on electrical wires is negligent. Keeping your puppy safe and secure in a crate with his toys is responsible pet management.

— Teoti Anderson of Lexington, S.C., past president of the Association of Pet Dog Trainers

Lay down a 6- to 12-inch layer of small, washed stone as a base. Rainwater will drain away, so you won't need to worry about muddy paws. It's easy to keep the area clean with poop-scoops, and you can also disinfect and deodorize the area. Every time you take him outside to go potty, whether on leash or carried (depending on the size of the pup), you should put him in this pen.

Note the tactile advantage: Your puppy will quickly associate the stones under his feet with why he's there, and there won't be many areas with that base that are off limits. Plus, your lawn (and carpets) will be spared. For now, it's his "puppy pen." When properly house-trained, your dog will continue to use this area as his bathroom for his entire life. Once he's mature and trained, you can leave the gate open so that he can go in and out on his own. However, there will still be times when you will want him safe and secure in that pen with the gate closed, so don't remove it.

Keep your puppy on a leash, or carry him to the area if he's never been on a leash before (or seems unsure about walking). When you set him down, keep

the leash loose and, if possible, out of his mouth. This is not playtime. Stand with him, moving him back and forth in a small area; 15 square feet is the maximum. If he's showing you how well he can sit, running a few steps may inspire him to get up. But you're not going anywhere. This is not a walk; it's "go potty" time.

As he is eliminating — and not a second later — praise him calmly saying "Good potty" (or whatever phrasing you've chosen to use every single time). This is his first lesson on where he is to relieve himself, and it is your first lesson on the essential matter of correct timing. For praise or for correction, timing is of the essence. The words you decide to use as praise will be the words you will be able to use in the future as a cue: "Go potty." Keeping the puppy on leash is important so he can't race off or play, but

Did You Know?

A well-stocked toy box should contain action, distraction and comfort toys. Action toys are anything that you can throw or roll to get your puppy moving. Distraction toys are durable items that make dogs work for their treats. Comfort toys are soft and stuffed, and they act like little security blankets.

NOTABLE & QUOTABLE

The first thing you should always do before your puppy comes home is to lie on the ground and look around. You want to be able to see everything your puppy is going to see. For the puppy, the world is one big chew toy.

— Cathleen Stamm, rescue volunteer in San Diego, Calif.

just as importantly, the leash keeps you beside him so you can get the essential "Good potty" cue timing right.

WELCOME HOME

Once your puppy has eliminated outside (he'll probably need to go after traveling in the crate from the breeder's house or rescue organization), he can be brought into his new home. However, you cannot — must not — just open the door and let him go out. He shouldn't have the freedom to run around wherever he wants at this stage (indoors or outdoors). Giving too much freedom too soon is at the top of the list of serious mistakes made by new puppy owners. Make sure he is still on leash or somewhere that someone can watch him every second. That way, you won't have to cope with soiled rugs, chewed-up shoes, gnawed furniture or other damage from an inventive puppy's method of housetraining. Those tiny, needle-sharp puppy teeth are weapons of mass destruction!

Here's more homework for you to complete prior to your puppy's arrival: You must decide which door you will use to take your puppy outside; then be sure all members of the family guard against the pup's access to all other doors.

Doors that open onto streets or an unfenced area are not safe for unleashed dogs of any age. Until they are trained to stay back, dogs find slipping out of open doors irresistible. This is a major reason for obedience training. If you have a yard, be sure it is securely fenced before you bring the puppy home, keeping in mind what his adult size and strength will be. If you do not have a yard and will have to take your dog for walks to relieve himself, plan to keep his leash in a handy place so you can attach it securely before you open the door to go outside.

Your next big decision will be determining which room will be the puppy's safe, happy and indestructible area of confinement. Be cautious about choosing a laundry room or a bathroom. When activated, a washer or dryer may terrify a puppy (or a dog of any age that has never encountered these modern, noisy marvels). Bathrooms often have to be shared by people who would probably prefer privacy to stepping on dog toys or in puppy puddles. Bathrooms also offer puppies amusing diversions such as towels to be chewed and toilet paper to be turned into streamers! Stripped of all those goodies, a spare bathroom might be your only solution, but use a pet gate (not a closed door) for two-way visibility.

The kitchen is usually the best choice. A pet gate, or baby gate, fitted across the kitchen doorway will keep the pup where he belongs, if you decide he will be safe

JOIN OUR ONLINE Club Pup™

Holidays are stressful enough without a new puppy around. However, you'll need to be especially diligent if you want your puppy to be safe during Halloween, Thanksgiving, Christmas and other celebratory occasions throughout the year. Go to **DogChannel.com/Club-Pup** and download special tips for avoiding *how*liday disasters.

in the entire kitchen area. You can also set up an exercise pen in the kitchen. This "X-pen" is a sturdy metal doggie version of a toddler's playpen. They are just as useful, come in various sizes and are sold in most pet-supply stores. Either way, your pup will be able to see what's going on around him and maybe even see into the next room, depending on your home's layout. Just as important: You can see him and catch his signals when he needs to go out. A solid, closed door shuts him out and begs to be scratched, gouged and eventually destroyed.

The kitchen area has several advantages over other areas of the house, such as:

◆ The floor is easily washable.
◆ It's where your dog's food is served.
◆ It's a good place to fit a crate.
◆ It's where people congregate and eat.

SHOPPING FOR YOUR PUPPY

As soon as you know which puppy (or older dog) you will be getting, there will be some shopping to do before you bring him home. The moment you walk in the pet-supply store, you'll be tempted in every direction, so here's a list of the essential things you'll need to get you and your puppy started.

Collars and Leashes: Canine collars are sized in inches, as well as according to breed size (small, medium, large, etc.). A soft, adjustable collar with a snap closure works well because puppies grow very quickly. Check the collar every week to be sure it's not getting too tight. (The test is two fingers' space between the collar and the pup's neck.) Collars come in almost every color, fabric and pattern you can imagine, but there's no need to go overboard when purchasing your pup's first one, because he will outgrow

it — and probably several replacements — in the next few months.

Do not buy a chain "choke" or "training" collar for a puppy. If, for some reason, you must have one for obedience training an older dog, be sure to remove it immediately after the training session is over. Never leave the training collar on the dog. The loose rings on these collars can easily catch on something and strangle a dog. Preferably, for an older new dog, you should consider a head collar or harness for housetraining and walks. (You should also remove these when you remove the leash.)

A 6-foot leash is best for housetraining, and you can even get one that matches the collar. Retractable leashes are handy for controlled exercise around the yard and for walks in the park, woods

Poison Control

If you suspect your puppy has ingested something poisonous, contact your veterinarian or a poison-control center for advice. Have the product label in-hand when you call, if possible.

If you and you can't get in touch with your vet right away, call one of several animal poison control centers immediately:

- **ASPCA Animal Poison Control Center:** 888-426-4435
- **National Animal Poison Control Center of the University of Illinois:** 900-680-0000 or 800-548-2423
- **Pet Poison Helpline:** 800-213-6680

Each of these helplines charges a fee for assistance, but it's certainly well worth it. The call could save your dog's life. If you take your dog to the vet or to an emergency veterinary hospital, be sure to bring some of the plant or product that you believe the dog might have swallowed. Keep an eye out for dangerous household products such as the following:

Traditional ethylene-glycol based antifreeze causes kidney failure. If you even suspect your puppy has ingested antifreeze, seek veterinary treatment within two to four hours in order to save her life.

Most rodent poisons contain warfarin, which is an anticoagulant that causes internal bleeding. Some other rodent poisons contain cholecalciferol, which deposits calcium in the blood vessels and causes kidney failure and other problems.

Weed killers, insect poisons and wood preservatives often contain arsenic. Ingestion causes abdominal pain, vomiting, bloody diarrhea and weakness, followed by kidney failure, collapse and death.

Lead, which can be found in paint, golf-ball coatings, putty and linoleum, causes abnormal behavior, unsteadiness, seizures, appetite loss, diarrhea and blindness.

Zinc (which can be found in pennies), zinc-oxide skin coating, calamine lotion, fertilizers and shampoos, causes the red blood cells to break down, resulting in lethargy, appetite loss, pale gums, brown urine, vomiting, diarrhea and sometimes death.

Iron-based rose fertilizers can cause kidney and liver failure. The toxic dose is 1 teaspoon of 5-percent concentration per 20-pound (9 kilogram) dog.

or country, once you have learned how to use it safely and correctly. (They are not recommended for city streets unless locked in the 4- to 6-foot range.)

Food and Water Bowls: Keep your pup's size and the amount of food he eats in mind when picking feeding and watering bowls; beyond that, the choice is a matter of personal preference. Design styles include weighted bowls that won't tip over (for strong, active or clumsy dogs), attractive or amusing ceramic ones (which can be easily broken), plastic ones in colors and prints (which can be chewed), or stainless steel. Stainless steel bowls are popular, for several reasons: They are unbreakable, easy to keep clean and durable. Before you bring your pup home, decide where you'll put his water bowl and food dish, and always keep them in the same place.

Food: The variety of dog food available today exceeds the brands of kids' cereals! The breeder or rescue organizer should provide you with a starter supply of the pup's current food; it's best to keep him on that puppy-formulated food. Shelters aren't usually financially able to feed top-quality dog food, so if your new addition to the family is from a shelter, ask your vet for suggestions and select the best food you can afford.

Good puppy food will make your housetraining easier because you're less likely to deal with upset tummies or disturbed digestive systems. Dogs (and puppies, in particular) generally prefer wet, canned meats mixed with dry kibble. Get a supply that will last you at least two weeks. Any necessary change in a dog's food must take place gradually, over a period of a week or more.

Crates: The size rule is that the crate must be big enough for the dog to stand up, turn around and lie down in when he is fully grown. Crates are often sized by breed or weight of the adult dog, which makes your selection easier. Some come with movable dividers to allow for a puppy's growth. Some include floors, while others feature floors that are sold separately. Save the fancy bedding for when your pup is housetrained.

While there are numerous varieties of crates made of manufactured fabrics, wood and thin plastic, two basic models are worth checking out. Closed (fiberglass) crates have wired doors and "windows" on the sides. The solid sides keep drafts out and feel more secure for puppies at night. They're also easy to clean, if your pup has an accident or gets carsick. The other type of crate is wire and therefore completely open. It's nice for the dog to see out (and for you to see in), but wire crates must be kept out of drafts and covered at night so the pup is not disturbed. Both fold up or come apart.

Exercise Pens (aka X-Pens): Exercise pens come with or without gates and in many circumferences, sizes and shapes, so

Collecting Samples

Urine or stool samples need to be fresh when your veterinarian examines them. "Fresh" means you'll need to collect a urine sample first-thing in the morning, before your puppy has eaten. It needs to be delivered to the veterinary office within an hour or two of your collection. You can pick up stool at any time of the day, but it's best not to refrigerate it. You don't want it to dry up.

To collect stool:

• Turn a resealable plastic bag inside out, and place it over your hand

• Pick up a small section of your pup's stool with the bag.

• Turn the bag right-side-out.

• Seal or tie it shut.

Or, pick up a small amount with a little shovel and place it in a clean food container with a lid, such as one for yogurt or cottage cheese.

To collect urine:

• Take your puppy outside on a short leash first thing in the morning.

• Put an aluminum foil pan or an old cookie sheet underneath your pup to catch the urine before it hits the ground.

• Pour the urine into a re-sealable plastic bag or food container with a lid.

you're sure to find one to fit your kitchen, yard, patio or wherever you intend to use it. The most important measurement is the height. A very small dog, or young puppy, may stay safely behind a 24–inch-high barrier, but a medium-sized dog will soon figure out how to climb over the top. For this reason, some pens are made with a bent edging of several inches to deter escapees. You can even get an X-pen with an opening designed to connect to a custom–fitted crate.

X-pens fold up, so they're easy to move. They come in metal, plastic and wood. Your choice could depend on how much of a chewer your pup might turn out to be.

Gates keep your puppy
in his proper place.

Beds: If you plan to keep your puppy in an X-pen or the kitchen, he will appreciate a soft bed in that space. Dog beds range from economy to luxury styles. The latter are not recommended for puppies who are not housetrained.

Grooming Tools: Regardless of your puppy's coat texture, he will need proper grooming at least once a week, or more often if his coat mats easily. It's best to acclimate your dog to a regular grooming routine while he is still young. You'll only need the basics at first: a brush and a comb suitable for your dog's coat, blunt-ended scissors for trimming unwanted hair and nail clippers for keeping his claws trimmed.

Don't forget about your dog's teeth. Human-grade toothpaste is harmful to dogs, but there are special dental products available for keeping your dog's teeth clean, so don't neglect these important grooming needs. More items such as canine shampoo, clippers and other special grooming tools will come later, depending on what you'll need to care for your adult dog's coat.

Toys: Pet-supply store toy departments seem endless and completely irresistible. Teething puppies (up to about 6 months of age) need two kinds of chew toys: the soft knotted-rope kind they can sink their teeth into and massage their gums with, and the indestructible hard rubber ones that challenge their jaws. Be sure the chew toys are compatible with your puppy's size. Both types of teething toys are great for retrieval toss games at playtime. You might consider getting your dog a furry pal of his own — a soft cuddly bedtime toy. That's enough toys for starters. You can succumb to buying more later on.

Treat-dispensing toys keep puppy minds active.

A variety of toys will keep your puppy happy and engaged.

Everything you do with your puppy is a very important part of his future training. It is important to remember that you must always begin your housetraining, and all other training, as you plan to continue; otherwise, you'll confuse your puppy.

After you've immediately taken your new pup to his designated potty area when you first bring him home, he's finally ready to go inside the house for the first time. Let him sniff around a room or two, but keep him on the leash so you can prevent him from going into off-limits areas or knocking over precious knickknacks. Then, let him explore his own safety zone (the kitchen or his X-pen), and offer him a toy — only one at first. You can give him more toys later, and he'll soon let you know which ones are his favorites.

The next milestone in your new puppy's life is his first meal. Always keep his water bowl available and refreshed. Before you put his food dish down, let him sniff the dish and lick a tiny amount of food from your fingers. It will prove to your puppy that you are indeed his "food fairy." It also helps prevent food aggression, which occurs when the dog won't let you near his food dish. Wait 15 or 20 minutes after he's finished before taking him out on his leash to his potty area, and walk him around that area until he goes. Again, praise as he eliminates.

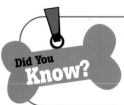

Did You Know?

Male puppies often don't lift their legs to urinate until they are nearly 6 months of age.

If you give ecstatic praise or treats when the puppy goes potty, he may try to make you happy by leaving a "present" where you least expect it — in the middle of your favorite rug, no doubt. And he'll be sitting nearby wagging his tail and waiting for a treat, too. Relieving himself is merely a natural response, not some fantastic trick you've taught him. You only need to let him know with a few quiet, kind words that you approve of what he's doing, while he does it and where he does it. Save the exuberant praise and treats to indicate your approval of other learned behaviors such as a correct response to his name and eventually to your "sit," "stay" and "come" cues.

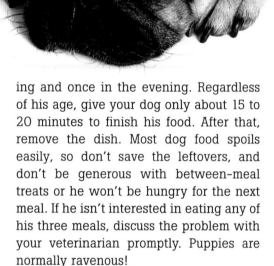

INTAKE AND OUTPUT

Stick to a tight schedule, and housetraining will go smoothly. Before and after play, before and after food, and before and after rest comes potty time! When your pup is fed at specific times, he'll also go potty at predictable times afterward — at least at *somewhat* predictable times! Leaving food down all day encourages all-day snacking, which defeats your role as his food provider and may lead to overeating and obesity. Moreover, you will never know exactly when he needs to relieve himself, and neither will he.

A normal routine for a puppy from about 10 weeks of age is to feed him three times a day — breakfast in the morning, lunch around noon and dinner no later than 5 p.m. That means a trip outside 15 to 20 minutes after each meal and once more before bedtime. That's in addition to the other potty pit stops every time he wakes up and after playtimes.

As your pup gets older, you can switch to feeding twice a day: once in the morn-ing and once in the evening. Regardless of his age, give your dog only about 15 to 20 minutes to finish his food. After that, remove the dish. Most dog food spoils easily, so don't save the leftovers, and don't be generous with between-meal treats or he won't be hungry for the next meal. If he isn't interested in eating any of his three meals, discuss the problem with your veterinarian promptly. Puppies are normally ravenous!

If any trip to his potty area is unsuccessful and you feel you've given him sufficient time, put your pup back in his confined area and try again in five to 10 minutes. During that time, closely watch him for any circling, whining or dashing about, as those are typical potty time signals. If you see any of the signals, pick him up, grab his leash and get him to his spot right away.

DAILY ROUTINE

Establishing your new young puppy's daily routine will consume most of your time, which is why it's important for someone to be home to do this initial

Just how quickly will your puppy grow? Go to Club Pup and download a growth chart. You also can see your pup's age in human years; the old standard of multiplying your dog's age by seven isn't quite accurate. Log onto **DogChannel.com/Club-Pup** and click on "Downloads."

Stick to a regular schedule when housetraining your new puppy. She'll need to go potty about once every hour — after meals, naps and play.

training. Taking the puppy out every time he wakes up, 15 to 20 minutes after every meal, and after every play session (inside or outside) usually works out to be about once every hour. Don't panic if your puppy has bowel movements up to six times a day; that's normal for some pups. But when he's down to two meals a day and has the physical ability to hold it, two or three bowel movements a day are more typical.

By taking your pup out on a leash and staying right with him, you will soon learn when he does what and how many trips he really needs. Consider writing it down if you need to; with so many trips, it's easy to forget. These "business trips" should not be leisurely walks around town. After he has relieved himself, give him some playtime either inside or outside, or allow him some time to explore (under your constant supervision, of course).

Here's another timing lesson: As you attach the leash, use a one-word cue to indicate where you and your puppy are heading. For example, say "Go potty" or say "Outside"

it's a
Fact

Sudden changes in diet and water sources often result in a puppy having digestive upset (i.e., loose stools).

If you've set a strict house-training schedule that your puppy just doesn't seem to be able to follow, have your veterinarian make sure the pup isn't suffering from an underlying health issue.

NOTABLE &
QUOTABLE

Medical and behavior problems can be responsible [for housetraining issues], so it helps to recognize what healthy stool looks like or to know when you need to change your training tactics. When in doubt, always check with your veterinarian, who will be able to tell if there's a problem.

— *Dana Bleifer, D.V.M., in Canoga Park, Calif.*

or whatever word you've chosen. Don't let the key word get lost in chitchat. Use only your key word. Be consistent, and he'll eventually run to the door when you say that word. Prior to that wonderful day, watch for those puppy signals of circling, whining or dashing about.

PAPERTRAINING

You may decide to papertrain your puppy or perhaps even train him to use a litter box in the house. Any small-breed puppy can be taught to use papers. People choose to papertrain for various reasons. Perhaps, at the start of a vacation period, you can't get your puppy to begin the outdoor housetraining process. Perhaps you can't find someone to come to your home during the day to give the puppy an afternoon potty break. Or perhaps you are a city dweller and outdoor training is too complicated, which may also be why you chose a small dog in the first place. There are also special canine litter boxes made for small dogs, but, as the puppy (especially a male) gets older and begins the instinctive ritual of kicking turf, those granules will fly, making a big mess!

If you have a toy-breed pup, you may choose to train him to relieve himself on newspapers or in a litter box throughout his life, but this is not recommended for dogs that will weigh more than 12 to 15 pounds at maturity. Whether or not you intend to train your puppy to use papers permanently, newspapers make a good safety net for at least the first few days; you can also find absorbent "puppy pads" at pet supply stores. Most puppies are fine with newspapers, but beware! Some puppies quickly discover what fun it is to turn paper into confetti. The choice must be yours, not your puppy's. Whatever your reasons, if papertraining is your plan, whether for those first few days or permanently, you need to start as soon as you bring the puppy into your home.

The beginning setup is the same as for all housetraining, so you'll need an exercise pen in the kitchen or the means to confine your pup there. Put several layers of newspaper in one corner of the X-pen, or pick an area that won't be in the family's footpath, if the puppy is loose in the kitchen with a pet gate. Do not paper the entire floor. The idea is to have the puppy go to the one small area that has the papers, not to encourage him to relieve himself anywhere.

For permanent papertraining, put the papers (or pads) in the area you will want him to continue to use — the kitchen or X-pen. When you see the signs that indicate

Did You Know?

Puppies that frequently lose control or dribble urine may have a strong ammonia-like odor. Your veterinarian can treat your puppy after determining what the underlying cause is. The doctor will want to know as much information as possible about the color and frequency of the urine you've observed at home. Normal urine should be yellow and clear (not cloudy), although certain drugs, such as buffered or coated aspirin, can turn the urine orange-yellow. If your puppy hasn't urinated in several hours, the urine will look thick because it's highly concentrated, and there won't be very much of it.

The Daily Routine

For successful housetraining, your puppy will need consistency. Have a prepared schedule to follow for the first couple of months.

- First thing in the morning: Potty. After four months of age, this can be followed by a walk.
- Breakfast by 8 a.m., then potty trip 15 minutes later.
- Nap time in her crate.
- As soon as she wakes up: Potty and playtime; possibly another potty trip after playtime.
- Lunch around noon followed by a potty trip 15 minutes later
- Nap time in her crate.
- As soon as she wakes up: Potty and playtime; possibly another potty trip after playtime.
- Nap time in her crate (At 12 to 16 weeks, this nap is replaced by a walk.).
- After she wakes up: Potty and playtime; possibly another potty trip after playtime.
- Supper around 5 p.m., then potty trip 15 minutes later.
- After the family's dinner: Playtime and a potty trip.
- Bedtime around 10 p.m.: One more potty trip, then into the crate for the night.

SMART TIP!

From the time your new puppy has her first bowel movement in your home, hopefully in your backyard, get in the habit of looking at the stool at least once a day to identify the color, consistency, odor and how often it happens. Ideally, the sample should be brown, firm, not overly smelly, and not occurring more often than about once or twice an hour or two to three times a day.

he needs to go, take him on leash to the papers and follow the same procedure that you would use if taking him outdoors. It may seem foolish to put the puppy on his leash in your kitchen, but you must take him to the paper spot you have chosen and then stay right with him until he goes. That means put him on leash for every potty trip! To reinforce the scent association, which will let the puppy know that this is his potty area, take a small portion of previously soiled newspaper and place it near a corner of the clean papers.

If they are merely to be used for emergencies, put the papers in one corner of the X-pen in the kitchen or near the door that you'll use to take the pup outside. Then, as he learns to use the papers and you see him head for them, take him outside — quickly! Keep the leash by the door or hooked to the X-pen so that you'll be ready. If you are too late, let him use the papers as you give him casual praise: Say "good pee" calmly and quietly.

Use this method if you plan to housetrain your pup to go outdoors only when you are at home and it's convenient to do so. He'll soon understand that papers are OK but outside is better. Again, you can transfer the scent by putting a bit of soiled papers in the area you want him to use outside. If newspapers are not for permanent use, eliminate them gradually by leaving a smaller piece each day until you're sure he no longer needs them. (Don't be too upset if there's an accident or two following their final removal — just forgive and forget.)

Even with a dog that is completely trained to relieve himself outdoors, if you started by papertraining, you can use newspapers throughout the dog's life whenever you have to be away longer than the adult dog might be able to hold it. Leave the papers by the dog's normal exit door and make no comment at all if they are used. When you get home, simply put the dog outside, roll up and discard the soiled papers, and disinfect the area.

Although some owners take full credit for the clever ways that they have trained their little puppies to go potty outside, the fact is that dogs prefer to eliminate outdoors and in the same area every time, so that they can leave — and pick up — scents as reference points. It's the old "I was here!" attitude that is common to many animals, not just dogs. Taking your puppy outdoors to the same spot every time is definitely the best and easiest way to housetrain him.

By now, you've noted how important it is to be consistent, and that applies most emphatically when it comes to the "one word" you'll use in housetraining. "Go potty" or "Go pee" — whatever wording you choose — all should be said as one word with the emphasis on the second syllable. This "one-word" mandate carries over into just about every single thing you'll be teaching your dog. From your dog's viewpoint, one specific word from you is connected to one specific action from him. You may end up amazed by your pup's vocabulary!

Did You Know?

Despite the most diligent housetraining efforts, many toy-breed puppies seem to take longer to housetrain and can be more of a challenge than their larger cousins. Their small bodies are so low to the ground that their owners have a hard time catching them in the act and correcting the behavior. Toy breeds also tend to have smaller bladders and may need to eliminate more frequently than large-breed pups. But contrary to what most people think, toy dogs are not hopeless to housetrain. To get the job done, take your small puppy out every 20 to 30 minutes for the first few weeks and be consistent about going out after meals, naps and playtimes.

DEN

Dogs are den animals, so think of a crate as your dog's very own den; don't ever think of it as a cage or a place for punishment. It's his special place for all-important undisturbed periods of sleep, his hideaway with a favorite toy and his place to escape what may sometimes be a busy world around him. A crate is where your dog will be safe when strangers are going in and out of your house, when excited kids are racing around, when you've just washed the floor or when you have to leave him alone for a couple of hours. It is also a useful tool for housetraining, once your new dog starts to get the basic idea, he won't eliminate in his crate.

DO NOT ENTER

Sometimes dogs become very possessive of their crates and don't want anyone invading their areas. This is an instance where, prevention is key. When teaching your puppy to return to his crate, occasionally put your hand into the crate and stroke his side or back, telling him what a good puppy he is. Occasionally, offer him a treat in his crate so he learns to allow you inside his hideaway.

it's a **Fact**

White vinegar is a good odor remover if you don't have a professional cleaner on hand; use one quarter cup of white vinegar to one quart of water when cleaning up potty accidents.

Children often get nipped when fooling around with a puppy in his crate, so kids need special warning and guidance. They must be warned to never try to crawl into a dog's crate, to never take anything out of the crate and to never try to pull the dog out of or push him into his crate. For all intents and purposes, the dog considers the crate his sanctuary.

This tendency toward possessive behavior is why it is generally not a good idea to feed your puppy in his crate. It can compel him to guard his food, which can lead to aggressive behavior around all food. Instead, teach him to sit before you put his dish on the floor; this tells him that you're the boss, as well as the food fairy.

The crate can be used to give your pup (or maybe you) quiet time when you are at your wit's end. However, never put him in his crate as punishment or when you are angry. He will begin to associate it as a bad place and getting him inside will be come increasingly more difficult. If he hides in his crate, he's only reacting to the anger in your voice, the scowl on your face or other negative body language. Instead, a timeout is given with the cue "crate." Use your pup's name, emphasize the word crate and speak in a reasonably firm — but never angry — tone of voice.

CRATE SIZE

Your dog's crate should be tall enough to allow him as an adult to stand up and turn around in, and long enough for him to lie down. If he's one of the giant breeds, a crate large enough to use through his puppy training will be fine, since he probably won't be using it later on. If your puppy will be medium to large when fully grown, you can get a crate appropriate for his adult size with a movable panel to adjust as necessary. The panel is used to create a smaller space for your puppy within the crate; if the crate is too large, the puppy will sleep at one end and use the other end as a bathroom. That is not what a crate is for!

A wide variety of crates is available, including wire (some fold for travel), high-impact fiberglass (easy to keep clean and accepted by most airlines), and soft fabric models (the latest thing for camping but not recommended for training, as they can be chewed and are not sturdy enough). There are even decorative crates made from rattan or polished wood that double as end tables. No one dares to think of those dog dens as "cages" now! Think of them more like elegant canine furniture.

A crate also has take-it-with-you convenience because anywhere you go can be your dog's home; even when you're away from home. Many hotels welcome dogs who are crated when left in the room alone — such as

Did You Know? There are many medical issues that can impede your housetraining efforts. A puppy may have a urinary-tract disorder if she seems to be in pain while urinating, if you see blood in the urine, or if she exhibits excessive urination or urinary incontinence. Young puppies can even have kidney disease. Puppies as young as 4 weeks of age can have bladder stones. If there are crystals in the urine, it will look cloudy. See your veterinarian if you notice any of these issues with your new pup.

NOTABLE & QUOTABLE

Sudden excitement can cause very loose stools, or sometimes, loose stools just mean the puppy has eaten something she shouldn't have, such as a dead animal, garbage or rich foods such as liver or meat, table scraps, sticks or grass. Often, the condition will clear up by feeding your puppy a few small meals that are easy on the stomach, such as cottage cheese or rice.

— Gary White, D.V.M., of Santa Anita Animal Hospital in Monrovia, Calif.

when you go out to dinner. A relative who is not keen on dogs won't object to your puppy's presence when he can stay crated during teatime or cocktail hour. Also, a crate will keep your dog safe in the car if you get in a fender bender or a worse accident. Even a very frightened dog can be removed to safety while still in his crate by anyone coming to your aid.

USING THE CRATE

The kitchen is generally the best place for your pup's crate. It's a hub of activity for people, so your puppy will learn that people come and go — and come back again. If the kitchen does not work for you for some reason, then keep the crate in whichever area you have chosen as his confined safe space. Never put your dog's crate in a secluded or empty room; this may seem like a comforting quiet space, but it will just make your pup feel neglected.

If you want your puppy to stay in your bedroom at night (or if the kids insist on having him in their room), either get a second crate or be prepared to move his crate from room to room. Even if you want your dog to sleep on your bed later on, it is unwise to let a puppy do so. If your pup jumps or falls off the bed, he could seriously injure the growth plates in his legs, which can do a lot of damage and possibly cripple him. You also don't

want him to wake up and start roaming around the room, where he could get into trouble or danger or perhaps go potty. Before moving the crate to your bedroom, consider that even your normal movements during the night could wake him, and of course he'll need to go potty … at 3 a.m. Enough said?

A TOOL FOR TRAINING

Now we come to the nitty-gritty task of cratetraining as a basic tool for housetraining. Most responsible breeders today give their pups at least an introduction to the crate in order to make the trips to their new homes less stressful. Some really good breeders let their pups sleep in crates for several nights before the new owners pick them up, which makes the owners' job a lot easier. If your breeder has been this considerate, show your appreciation.

Put the crate in the designated area and leave the door open. For starters, use an old folded towel to line the floor of the crate (do not use newspapers). Nice bedding comes

it's a Fact

As a general rule, a puppy should only be left in her crate for as many hours as she is months old. So a 4-month-old puppy should not be left in her crate for more than 4 hours straight.

JOIN OUR ONLINE
Club Pup™

Before you bring your puppy home, make sure you don't have anything that can put her in harm's way. Go to Club Pup and download a list of poisonous plants and foods to avoid. Log on to **DogChannel.com/Club-Pup** and click on "Downloads."

later, when your puppy is truly house-trained. If you're using a wire crate, drape a towel, blanket or fitted cover over it at night, leaving the front panel uncovered. This eliminates drafts and lets your pup have a slightly dark place to sleep. Add a safe, soft toy for him to cuddle up with and a safe chew toy for teething, and you have created a puppy haven.

Introduce your pup to where his crate will normally be located upon arrival to his new home — of course, after he has eliminated outside and has had a few minutes to inspect the areas in which he is allowed. To lure him into his crate, show him a toy and, while holding it in your hand, let him follow it into the crate as you say "crate" in a happy voice. Then lure your pup out of the crate, using the toy as bait. After a few repetitions of this in-and-out routine, show him a small treat and toss it into the crate when he shows an interest.

As his head goes into the crate (not a second before or after), say "Crate! Good dog!" in your happiest voice. Don't expect success all at once, when you've just walked in the door. This training practice should be repeated over the next two weeks, or more, until he follows your guiding hand (eventually without a treat) as you say "crate." During these brief training

Cratetraining will prevent your dog from taking over your bed!

periods, the crate door should remain open. Again, all of this is to get your pup to work with you and to provide a good foundation for future obedience training.

After four or five successful times going into the crate, and when your pup seems comfortable with the idea, close the door for a few minutes. Move away and pretend to be busy somewhere else in the room. Do not let him out if he is whining or fussing. Wait until he is quiet, then open the crate door. Open it without any comment or any sign of a joyous reunion. You don't want him to associate your approval with his leaving his crate; you want him to make that positive connection only when he does as he's told and goes into it. For now, say "Crate! Good dog!" as he goes in and stay silent as he comes out.

If your pup is crated in your bedroom at night and he fusses, tap on the top of the

Did You Know? Submissive urination is not a housetraining issue. It occurs when your pup pees a little every time she greets someone. This has to do with normal canine behavior that can, and should, be dealt with in a positive way.

6 Steps to Successful Cratetraining

1. Tell your puppy "crate," and place her in the crate with a toy or small treat (a piece of cheese or a morsel of a biscuit). Let her stay in the crate for five minutes while you are in the same room. Then release her and praise lavishly. Never release her when she is fussing. Wait until she is quiet before you let her out.

2. Repeat step 1 several times a day.

3. The next day, place the puppy in the crate as before. Let her stay there for 10 minutes. Do this several times.

4. Increase the time intervals in five-minute increments until your puppy stays in her crate for 30 minutes with you in the room. Always take her to her relief area after prolonged periods in her crate.

5. Now go back to step 1 and let the puppy stay in her crate for five minutes; this time leave the room.

6. Once again, increase the time in five-minute increments. When your puppy stays willingly in her crate (she may even fall asleep!) for 30 minutes without you in the room, she will be ready to stay in it for several hours at a time.

crate (not too hard) but don't say anything. If you say even short things like "Go to sleep," "It's OK" (which it definitely isn't) or "Quiet," your pup will consider whatever you say as your part of the "fussy" conversation he started. In his mind, it's a "gotcha!" A bop or two on the crate should get him to settle down. If you're a nighttime TV viewer, keep the volume lower than usual, and that may help him fall asleep.

If your puppy's crate remains in the kitchen overnight, which is the preferred location, then begin a routine his first night home.

Take him on his last trip outside, turn the lights out and keep the house quiet. This will signal the pup that it is bedtime, and he'll eventually settle down. If he fusses, one sharp "Quiet!" from another room is your one and only response. Don't return to visit him or say anything more if he fusses. He'll soon learn that when you say "Good night," the rest of the message is "See you in the morning."

Yes, housetraining's main goal is getting your puppy to potty in the preferred location. It also, however, means teaching him about his new home and the people who share it with him – especially children. Puppies and children need to be taught to act appropriately with each other, and your house needs to be prepped for your puppy as you would prepare for a baby. That means you need to tidy up all those areas that you know to avoid but a puppy will only find interesting, at the cost of his own safety.

DON'T KID AROUND!

Dogs and kids are a wonderful, natural combination. They have lots of unspoken things to offer each other, but both require adult supervision.

Never leave any dog alone with an infant or toddler. If the baby does anything that the dog doesn't like or doesn't understand, the dog could snap or even bite, no matter how

Did You Know? **Teaching your puppy to maneuver through a doggie door requires little training,** assuming she's large enough to apply the necessary pressure to open it. Initially, hold the door open and lure her back and forth with a treat. Gradually, hold the door open less and less, until she learns to push through herself. Most pups seem to enjoy the "game" and catch on very quickly.

sweet-tempered the dog may otherwise be. Toddlers bite, too, and a dog's ears are often the target! It's important that 2- and 3-year-olds understand that not every dog is friendly because, at that age, they often want to rush up and throw their arms around every dog's neck. Even a sweet or shy dog might bite. Dogs generally don't appreciate being tackled by small strangers!

It will be ineffective to scream "Don't touch the dog!" at a toddler (especially if the child is already racing toward the dog). Prevent the situation entirely by introducing the toddler to a dog who you know is calm and friendly and who is on leash with his owner present. Teach the child how to hold out a hand for the dog to sniff. The toddler will probably giggle at being tickled and pull his hand away, which is a perfectly normal reaction.

Teach slightly older children never to tease dogs. Dogs do not understand teasing of any kind as fun, and having to deal with kids' teasing can turn a nice dog into

Children's faces should not be up in your puppy's face. Even a little dog might accidentally bite if he feels uncomfortable.

an aggressive one. Take the time to teach the kids in your life how to behave with a dog — any dog, not just yours. Even if they have owned dogs before, teach them that dogs are individuals and should be treated as such.

Teasing puppies is especially risky. Just feel those sharp puppy teeth! One of the first things kids must learn is that puppies do not have hands. Sound weird? If a child chooses to tease a pup with one of his toys, the dog will eventually take his toy back with his teeth. A child's hands can easily get caught in the middle. The pup is not intentionally biting, just taking back what the child took.

FACE THE PROBLEM

It may look cute in pictures, but babies' and children's faces do not belong next to dogs' faces. Again, your puppy could nip in reaction to a small child's unintentionally clumsy movements. These things can happen very quickly; the baby screams and the dog may be wrongly punished. Pups may lick an adult's face or hands out of respect or dominance, but a puppy may view a child the same way he views his littermates, and puppies "play" with their mouths.

It is also not a good idea to let a child pick up a puppy or small dog. Being carried around (and possibly dropped) is unnatural to a dog, and squeezing is not the same as a hug. Furthermore, since snacks in a child's hand are an easy target for an always-hungry pup. When it's snack time for the children, give your puppy his own snack, preferably in his crate.

All of these warnings serve to point out that children need to be taught to respect the puppy's place in the home — and the sooner, the better. As puppies grow into full-sized dogs, they will become stronger, so it's important to teach children early. These

Keep an eye on your child and puppy while they play together. Neither one knows how to play gently enough without accidentally hurting or scaring the other.

warnings also reinforce the fact that, when it comes to kids and dogs in the same home or on the same turf, owners need to be cautious and vigilant about supervision.

HOME CONSIDERATIONS

Throughout your home lurk many dangers for your dog. The garage is especially dangerous because there are a lot of obvious, and some not so obvious, things that dogs should avoid. Sweet-tasting antifreeze is lethal, and just about everything we use in our gardens, on sidewalks and driveways, and in cars can be harmful. Containers of these toxic chemicals may leak, fall off shelves or just lie forgotten on the floor. If you don't pay attention to securing them out of your dog's reach, the consequences could be very serious and even deadly.

Cocoa mulch contains theobromine (which is also in chocolate), an ingredient that is lethal to dogs and cats. Most weed killers and

JOIN OUR ONLINE Club Pup™

The best way to get your puppy well socialized is to introduce her to different kids of people and situations: Have her meet a man with a beard, take her to a dog-friendly restaurant, take her for a ride in the car. Go online to download a socialization checklist at **DogChannel. com/Club-Pup**

Dangerous plants and pesticides might be lurking in your back-yard, so make sure your puppy steers clear of your flower bed.

pesticides and even some fertilizers are poisonous to pets, as are quite a few types of plants dogs love to dig up. Many houseplants such as ivy, poinsettia and philodendron are deadly, too. In the garden, foxglove, hydrangea and chrysanthemum can be fatal to puppies. A full list of toxic plants can be found in the Animal Poison Control Center of the American Society for the Prevention of Cruelty to Animals' website, www.aspca.org.

it's a Fact

In roughly half of male dogs, behaviors such as urine marking, mounting and fighting decrease or disappear after neutering, but it can take several weeks before you see a change. Almost all male dogs stick closer to home after they're neutered.

To safeguard your pup for his entire life, lock all chemicals in secure cabinets so your dog cannot get into them, and limit their use. If you have toxic plants in your home or yard, you don't necessarily have to get rid of them, but you do have to puppy-proof them. Restrict your dog's access to areas containing these plants, or block the plants off with chicken wire or with netting. As an added safety measure, you can spray suspicious plants in the yard and home with one of the foul-tasting dog-training products sold to deter pets from chewing.

POOL PROTECTION

Puppies are not born swimmers. They cannot just jump into a river, lake or pool and swim! Some dogs like being in water, and some definitely do not. No dog, however, can safely swim any distance naturally — not even the water-retrieving breeds (although, granted, they are quicker to learn).

NOTABLE & QUOTABLE

[The crate] must be small so the pup cannot mess in it without laying in it. This will stop most dogs from crate-messing. When they wake up or after playing or eating, they should be taken outside and told to go pee. As soon as they do, they should be praised and given a small treat — a small bit of something good like a hot dog. — dog breeder Shannon Larson of Brooks, Canada

SMART TIP!

Finding — and cleaning up after — doggie diarrhea is not pleasant, but repeatedly discovering healthy-looking poop on the same spot on the rug after you think your puppy is housetrained isn't much better. Your puppy might be doing this because the area has a familiar smell and she feels safe there. To dissuade your puppy from choosing this location, put her food dish in this location and feed her there. Puppies usually won't soil where they eat. You'll also need to redouble your housetraining efforts. If you can't watch your puppy, put her into her crate or an enclosed area.

On their own, dogs learn to swim by wading into the water until their feet stop touching the bottom; then they turn around and "dog paddle" back. This gradual procedure is not possible in a pool. When your puppy is at least six months old, you can teach him to swim by holding him securely around his ribs or under his chest at the shallow end of the pool to allow him to get comfortable with paddling and staying afloat.

Providing your dog with a safe, easy and clearly visible means of getting out of the pool is essential. You may have to buy a ramp and teach him exactly how to use it in order to get out of the water. Never leave a dog alone near a pool — even when the pool is covered. Dogs drown very easily. If your dog hates the water, get him a life

Puppies don't instinctively know how to swim, and a backyard pool can be just as dangerous to a puppy as to a child. Supervise your dog's exercise time and teach him to exit the pool safely if he falls in.

Everyone in the household must be on the same page and must stick to the [housetraining] routine no matter what. I had to train my husband not to let our dog out of the crate because he felt sorry for her. So I had to train him to train her, and I had to keep an eye on both of them! — dog owner Dianna Starr of Bisbee, Ariz.

SMART TIP!

To direct your puppy to eliminate at rest stops and other places when you're traveling, let her know the time and place to potty. This will be easy if you teach your dog a "go-potty" cue. Pick a word or phase to use whenever you take your dog to a potty area. Choose something you won't be embarrassed to say out loud around strangers because you'll be using it at rest areas, parks and other public places. Some suggestions for cues are "go potty," "get busy," "hurry up" or "eliminate." Pick one cue and stick with it, so your dog will learn that it always means the same thing.

jacket for times when you'll be around water. A life jacket is mandatory for canine boating enthusiasts.

Some breeds — the Portuguese Water Dog and the Irish Water Spaniel, for example — were especially bred to work in the water with fishermen. If you have one of these special "water-working" breeds, read up on how they are safely trained.

CAR SAFETY

It doesn't take a heat wave for a warm car to be a death trap for a dog. A dog's normal body temperature is near 102 degrees Fahrenheit, and dogs don't sweat. They pant to breathe in cool air. The temperature inside a car — even when parked in the shade with the windows left partially open — can escalate dramatically in a matter of minutes. Most dogs left in this situation die of heatstroke or suffer brain damage before they can be rescued. Never leave a dog in a car — loose or crated — on a day that is the least bit warm, even when you think you'll only be gone for a few minutes.

The other part of car safety for your dog is the use of a properly secured crate or, possibly, a backseat barrier. Another available safety device is a canine seat belt that buckles onto the car's seat-belt system. Also, never let your dog put his head out the car window while you're driving. A major cause of eye damage in dogs is from road dust in the eyes.

CITY FOLKS

If you live in a metropolitan area, you may have to carry your puppy in and out of elevators or up and down stairs. Never put a puppy on the floor of an elevator where he could be stepped on or be frightened by the sound or action of people getting on and off. If you must use an elevator and

Gradually teach your puppy to walk on stairs, and set up a pet gate if he's prone to playing near them.

your dog is too big for you to hold, put him down in a corner and stand guard. Don't get into a crowded elevator.

Stairs are a problem for all young puppies. Get down on your hands and knees at the top of a flight of stairs and you'll see why. It's pretty scary! Most pups will attempt the Superman tactic and take a flying leap from the top, which often results in injury — sometimes even causing irreparable damage. Teach your pup how to go down stairs safely. Start at the bottom, not the top. If your puppy is large enough to go down the last step, stand in front of him and ease him down the last two. When he can handle that, gradually (over a period of many weeks) add one step at a time, still standing in front of him to prevent a leap. But keep in mind that he may always leap off that last step. Remember, stairs are just as dangerous to puppies as they are to toddlers. You might need to use a pet gate at the top (or bottom) of your staircase to keep your pup safe.

Did You Know?

Most male dogs (and some females, too) like to mark their territory with urine. This instinct serves to let other dogs know, by the individual's scent, who has been there. At home, dogs usually mark repeatedly at certain points in their yard or along their daily walking route. Each time your dog goes by those spots, she'll check for other dogs' urine marks and leave a new pee-mail message of her own.

TRAINING

Training your puppy is an around-the-clock task, and regardless of his age, his likes, his dislikes and his previously learned habits (in the case of an older rescued dog), you both need to learn how to best create a life together. Learning how to incorporate training with an appropriate balance is key. Although you are the boss, don't be too bossy. You are the food fairy, but overfeeding causes tummy aches and obesity. You are also the "treat trader," which can become tough to control. Remember: Training is an around-the-clock job. Keep up with it at all costs; don't let your dog train you!

Everything you do and say, and how you do and say it, affects puppy training. To be most effective, training requires consistent, good-natured patience. To a dog, human language sounds like it is from another planet! Until your pup can make the connection between the cue and what you expect him to do when you say it, he's only hearing sounds. For this reason, never use conversational tones when training your dog. For example, saying "Come on, sweetie, be my good little baby and sit like a good boy" is verbal garbage to your dog. Not to mention that it is totally confusing if, by chance, he should happen to catch the word "good" attached to his name. Keep cues short, simple and consistent for best training results.

Also, remember to keep your puppy's name associated only with positive experiences. Your puppy should always associate his name with something you ask him to do, followed by your approval if he does right. If he doesn't get it right, he just hasn't understood, so try again or ask him to do some-

SMART TIP!

If you have to travel to pick up your puppy, use the crate in the car as her safety seat on the trip home. (It's much nicer than having a carsick pup in your passenger's lap!) Never let your small-to medium-size dog travel in the car without her crate. If she's a big dog when you get her, or if she outgrows the crate, install a protective barrier to keep her safely in the rear of the vehicle.

thing he does understand. Say your dog's name, then "Sit," and when he does, add "Good boy!" with a big smile.

All corrections should be made without his name. Say: "Leave it!" (no name). It's just a warning, so you don't need to sound like a drill sergeant. "Uh-uh" is another good warning sound. For an especially firm correction, you can use something that sounds more like a dog bark.

Stop and think for a minute how confusing the word "no" must be to a dog. We use it constantly in conversation. "You know what?" "No way will I do that!" "There's no milk!" You get the picture. Instead of "no," try saying something that is not a word but that your puppy will interpret as "knock it off!" Say "Aacht!" in a growly voice and with a scowling face when you've caught him in the act. This also works as a warning signal, sometimes better than the cue "Leave it."

Language is confusing to dogs. This could be what makes them so observant. They pick up on our body language and our reactions to things like doorbells, telephones and so on. They quickly figure out the difference between what their owners wear when it's time to go for a walk and what they wear to work. And they learn to tell time; they know when everyone is about to leave the house, and they anticipate everyone's return.

PLAN B

Consistency, supervision and positive reinforcement are the keys to housetraining a puppy. If you stick to the plan, you should get results. But what if you have done everything "by the book" and are still not getting any results?

First, identify the reason, but don't jump to hasty conclusions about housetraining lapses. A wide range of simple issues can explain housetraining failures. Misunderstanding the cause will result in unproductive attempts to correct the problem — which can potentially make matters worse. Start by ruling out the most obvious possibilities first.

If your puppy is having problems learning housetraining, find out what the cause is. Ask yourself these questions.

1. Have there been any recent changes in your dog's routine? Is he being exercised in a new location or on a different sur-

Did You Know?

Some puppies have the disgusting habit of eating their own excrement, which is called *coprophagia*. The most common reason they do this is because they have underdeveloped digestive systems that allow undigested food to pass through their systems. They think this food is a treat because they don't have the same social taboos about eating feces that we do. If your pup is eating poop, take her to the veterinarian for a consultation. Products are available to add to your puppy's food to make the feces distasteful, but these may or may not do the trick. To be safe, pick feces up in the yard as soon as your puppy relieves herself. Don't scold or make any other corrections because this often backfires and causes a housetraining problem.

face? Don't overlook treats, snacks or the neighbor's cat food when investigating possible dietary changes.

2. Is there any reason for you dog to feel threatened, intimidated or encouraged to display dominant behavior toward another person or pet? Adolescence is a common trigger for a puppy's housetraining lapses. But these hormonal changes can also provoke adult dogs to mark territorially.

3. Do any events coincide with the onset of the problem, such as a sudden change in the weather or the presence of workmen, gardeners or new neighbors? Have you recently increased or decreased your dog's territory in your home?

4. How do family members typically respond to your dog's housetraining lapses? Human reactions to the situation can make matters worse. For instance, even the most diligent housetraining can be ineffective if one family member berates the dog or fails to reinforce the routine.

5. Are you scrupulous about cleaning up accidents? A dog's olfactory receptors trigger nerve endings in his bladder, which is why sniffing is a major indicator of a dog's need to urinate. Dogs can distinguish traces of odor undetectable to humans. Ineffective clean-up will only lure the dog back to the scene of the crime; it may also encourage other pets to relieve themselves in that spot.

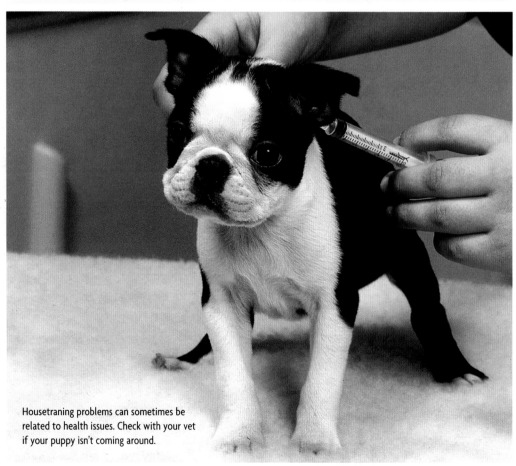

Housetraning problems can sometimes be related to health issues. Check with your vet if your puppy isn't coming around.

Canine Development Schedule

It is important to understand how and at what age a puppy develops into adulthood. Consult the following canine development schedule to determine the stage your puppy is currently experiencing. This will help you work with your puppy in the weeks and months ahead.

Stages One to Step Three: Birth to 7 Weeks

A young puppy needs food, sleep and warmth; she will respond to simple and gentle touching. She needs her mother for security and discipline, and her littermates for learning and social interaction. She will learn to function within a pack and to learn the order of dominance. Begin socializing young puppies with adults and children for short periods. This is also the stage when the puppy begins to become aware of her environment.

Stage Four: 8 to 12 Weeks

The pup's brain is now fully developed. This is when she needs to socialize with the world. She can now be separated from her mother and littermates; she needs to change from canine pack to human pack. Human dominance is necessary so the pup can learn her place in your family pack.

Stage Five: 13 to 16 Weeks

This is the stage when the puppy begins the change into adolescence. Now is when training, socialization and formal obedience should begin. Start to introduce your dog to more experiences and different types of people, places and situations. Be firm and fair. Your puppy's flight (and other fearful) instincts may be prominent, but permissiveness and over-disciplining can do permanent damage. Always praise for good behavior.

Stage Six: 4 to 8 Months (Juvenile)

Your puppy may enter another fear period in this stage. It usually passes quickly, but be aware of your puppy's fear and pain, and never force her to do something that she does not want to do. Introduce her to new situations slowly and with lots of treats. Sexual maturity is reached in this stage, and dominant traits can be established if you dog is not properly trained and socialized. Your puppy should, at the very least, understand the basic cues of sit, down, come and stay.

Note: These are approximate time frames. Allow for individual differences in puppies.

6. Could it be a medical issue? Medical conditions known to compromise bowel or bladder control include infections, inflammatory disease, parasites, kidney or bladder stones, colitis, cancer, diabetes and neurological disorders. Some medical problems can lead to housetraining lapses although the cause-and-effect relationship is not immediately obvious. For instance, a dog suffering from degenerative joint disease or failing eyesight may become reluctant to venture outdoors. Be prepared to provide your vet with detailed information about variations in the dog's normal elimination patterns, such as when you first noticed the problem, where and when the housetraining lapses occur, and whether the dog has exhibited any concurrent physical or behavioral changes.

7. If a vet exam doesn't provide an answer, investigate psychological motives. This gets more complicated because canine perceptions are a combination of environment and genetics. Dogs of every age constantly revise their behavior in response to changes in their surroundings, and subtle changes may easily escape your notice. Evaluate every aspect of your dog's routine to pinpoint the source of the problem

If that doesn't bring you any closer to an answer, reexamine your expectations about the process. Housetraining is a combination of mental and physical conditioning. A dog's mental and physical abilities to conform to a housetraining routine are subject to great variation. Rather than a revised plan, patience and persistence may be the solution.

it's a Fact

Dogs are pack animals. As puppies, they play together and sleep together; as they mature, they almost always choose to have company rather than go off somewhere alone. Generally, most dogs follow the members of their families from room to room, or they at least stay someplace where they can see most rooms in the house. This desire for company helps housetraining in at least two ways. First, it builds a bond between you and your dog that makes her want to please you and work with you. Second, your dog's proximity enables you to see where she is and what she's doing — which is crucial to preventing doggie bathroom accidents.

You don't have to feel alone when housetraining issues arise. Ask other dogs owners for advice and tips by logging on to **Dog Channel.com/Club-Pup** and clicking on "Community." Current dog owners who have succeeded in housetraining will be able to give you tips, pointers and encouragement.

HERE'S TO SUCCESS

Success that comes by luck is usually short lived. Success that comes by proven methods is often more easily achieved and is more permanent. If you follow the procedures in the previous chapters, you and your puppy will be housetrained in no time.

For easy housetraining, keep in mind that you should begin cratetraining your puppy as soon as you bring him home. A puppy isn't likely to go to the bathroom in his crate. If you don't want him going inside the house, don't train him to use newspaper or puppy pads, even in the beginning. Skip that stage and proceed outdoors right away. Otherwise, he will always return to that area indoors.

Your puppy will train quickly if you are disciplined about keeping an eye on him and not letting him out of your sight. Follow these basic steps for quick housetraining:

1. Choose an area in the yard you want your puppy to recognize as the potty location.

2. Any time your puppy wakes up or after meals and playtime, attach a leash to his collar and take him to the designated potty location. By using a leash, your puppy can't run through the yard to play and will learn that this is potty time.

3. Remain with your pup in the same spot until he pees or poops. When your puppy is done sniffing that area or even before, he will go to the bathroom. Don't walk to a new location if the puppy doesn't go right away because your pup will want to sniff that area before going.

4. Use your chosen elimination cue, such as "go potty."

5. As your puppy goes potty, praise him lavishly.

6. The next step is to bring your puppy back into the house.

7. Repeat the above process every 20 to 30 minutes.

8. If you see your puppy sniffing the floor and walking in circles, take him outside to go potty immediately.

9. If you cannot watch your puppy for some reason, put him inside his crate.

10. When you let your puppy out of the crate, immediately take him outside.

Clearly, most dogs are willing, even eager, to learn proper potty protocol. Their instincts are for cleanliness and routine; they want to keep their dens clean, they learn through repetition and they want to bond with their people. All you need to do is to take the right approach to capitalize on those instincts.

To train your dog successfully, take a moment to view the world from your puppy's perspective. Think positively, pay attention and be consistent. Because dogs learn faster with repetition, consistency is a crucial weapon in your arsenal of housetraining techniques. By taking your pup to his potty spot at the same times each and every day, you teach him to anticipate those potty breaks — and to hold it until breaktime. Consistency helps make your pup's good bathroom manners a habit that he won't need to break. And because he

Did You Know?

Putting a young puppy (or new adult dog) in the basement or garage when you are not at home may backfire. Dogs are tactile creatures. They use their feet as sensors, and a puppy kept on concrete will associate that touch with relieving herself — on sidewalks, on the patio or around the pool!

Solving Submissive Urination

Puppies who may be house-trained but who urinate a little when they greet you or a stranger aren't misbehaving, they're anxious, scared or intimidated. Your pup may also dribble urine if you bend over to pick her up or if you yell at her. To stop it from happening:

1 Don't become upset. This will make things worse.

2 Keep homecoming greetings low-key and avoid big hoopla welcomes. An insecure puppy doesn't understand this kind of greeting and wants to get on your good side by groveling (and peeing).

3 Without saying a word, toss your pup a treat as soon as you walk in the door and ignore the dog until she approaches you.

4 When your puppy comes over to you, kneel down and rub her chest a few times.

5 Don't reach over your puppy's head to say hello. This gesture can be intimidating to an insecure, submissive dog. Just say "hello" in a happy voice.

6 Take your puppy to obedience classes and teach her a few easy behaviors such as sit, stay, stand, down and come, to build her confidence so she can earn your praise. This way, your pup can show her devotion to you without having to grovel for it.

wants to please you, once he understands what you expect of him, he won't want to let you down!

FROM HOUSETRAINING TO TRAINING

Obedience is what you teach your dog from the minute you pick him up from the breeder (or rescue center). It continues from housetraining all the way to training agility, lure coursing, retrieving or whatever else you have in mind down the road. At 5 or 6 months of age, when you first attend obe-

dience classes, what you learn in class must be incorporated throughout your daily routine. Practice, practice, practice!

Here are some ways to incorporate basic obedience into your everyday routine: As you approach a doorway, your dog should sit, then follow as you go through. On the street corner, your dog should do a "sit-stay" on your cue while you check traffic; when you step off the curb, he should heel beside you. When you prepare your dog's dinner, he should sit and patiently wait until you put down his dish and tell him it is OK to start eating. Praise you dog every step of the way to encourage good behavior.

Eventually, you can teach your dog a variety of words, although consistency in tone and meaning is important (remember that even if a cue consists of two words, say it as a unit). Saying "flowers" with a glare means "Don't you dare lift your leg on my pansies!" "Fetch," "carry" and "find it" each have specific meanings and will increase your dog's skills and vocabulary. People are always amazed at how many words a dog can learn, and it's all done one word at a time with a lot of patience! Some cues are for fun and some are for safety. While "roll over" or "high five" are fun tricks, knowing "come" and "stay" could save your dog's life.

Rewards are an important part of training, but food rewards should be very, very small. This is not the time for your puppy to lie down and enjoy an entire dog biscuit. Just give a taste for him to quickly swallow so his attention will be back on you and the training session. He thinks he's paying attention to get more treats, but you know it's for more training. Remember that you're the treat trader; treats don't come for free!

NOTABLE & QUOTABLE

Arousal/increased activity of your dog caused by anxiety can bring about defecation and urination. Dogs with separation anxiety may eliminate regularly whenever the person to whom the dog is attached is physically separated from the dog. Fear of noises, outside objects or an animal can cause a dog to refuse to go outdoors to eliminate. Some dogs refuse to leave the porch if it is raining or snowing, thus not eliminating when given the opportunity. Some dogs refuse to go in the presence of their owner. — Karla Gardner Hamlin, a certified pet dog trainer

COMMUNICATION

Your dog's education is your responsibility, but, before you can obedience train your puppy, you'll need to understand how he thinks and communicates. You can't teach him our language without first knowing his.

BODY TALK

To be an effective teacher, you need to recognize your puppy's body language, vocal tones and other clues; plus, you'll need to understand basic canine social behavior and structure. What is your dog saying when he barks with his ears pricked forward and tail held high? Is your puppy being aggressive when he pounces and jumps around? When you see his teeth, is he showing you that he's about to bite?

There are nuances to all of these behaviors and postures that have very different meanings. Just because you see a dog's teeth does not mean he's ready to bite you. He might be "smiling," which is a very common greeting behavior in puppies and submissive dogs. When your puppy greets you

it's a Fact
Nothing is accomplished by screaming, physical violence, holding a grudge, verbal reasoning or arguing. These behaviors are not part of canine communication. They are purely human reactions based on the human emotion of frustration. Speak "canine," and your puppy will understand you.

with a toy, he's not doing it merely because he wants to play; rather, he's presenting the toy to you as his pack member — sharing his possession.

Once you are able to interpret canine language, you can teach your puppy to interpret your language. Dogs can learn the meanings of hundreds of words and signals. They are always open to learning new things, so the only limitation to your puppy's vocabulary is your own time and imagination.

CANINE BODY LANGUAGE

Here's a basic outline of canine communication, from ears to tails. When you fully understand what your puppy is expressing, you'll have the edge you need to train him effectively.

Ears: Ears pricked forward means that the dog is alert and zeroing in on something. The alert stance can indicate a form of dominance or just an interest in something. An alert dog may choose to go toward the object of interest, so be ready to contend with this.

Ears held with their openings to the sides means that the dog is paying attention. When the ears are held lazily at the sides, it means that the dog is relaxed. However, it can also mean that the dog is getting tired. When you see the ears in this position, it's time to end the training session.

Ears held slightly back may mean that the dog is listening or may signal a slight form of submission. This dog is paying attention to you but may respond meekly. Try making your tempo and attitude a little more upbeat to increase your puppy's enthusiasm.

When the ears are held flat to the head, it's a definite signal of submission and/or fear. A dog who bites out of fear will hold his ears flat to his head. It means your puppy is scared of something. Try to encourage him, instead of punish him.

Offer more praise, and reward more frequently for smaller goals.

To read the body language of a dog with folded or hanging ears, look at the bases of his ears — where his ears attach to the head. The bases will move in telltale ways to signal the dog's mood.

Head: A head held high means interest or alertness to a stimulus. It can also signal an assertive personality. Be ready to respond to your puppy's desire to investigate. A head held at a relaxed angle — not high or low — indicates, of course, a relaxed dog. He's a willing partner, attentive and happy.

The head held with the eyes pointing down shows a submissive dog or one who wishes to avoid a confrontation. When you see this, be more encouraging and enthusiastic to decrease any intimidation that your puppy is experiencing.

When a dog holds his head low and stretches his neck forward, he is engaging in a very submissive greeting gesture that is

You might not be able to read your pup's mind, but that doesn't mean you can't learn to understand each other. Pay attention to your dog's body language, as well as his different types of verbalizations, and you'll soon be able to decipher what he's telling you.

JOIN OUR ONLINE
Club Pup™

You have an unbreakable bond with your dog, but do you always understand her? Find out what your puppy is saying when she barks, howls or growls. Go online and download "Dog Speak," which outlines how dogs communicate. Go to **DogChannel.com/Club-Pup** and click on "downloads."

common in puppies and submissive dogs. When you see this posture, allow the dog to come to you. Lure him with a toy or treat; entice him with a pleasant tone of voice. Never go directly to him; he will perceive this as further intimidation, not reassurance.

Eyes: The eyes say a lot. To a dog, direct eye contact is a dominant gesture. If a dog stares directly into your eyes without looking away, be aware. This is a very assertive animal. A dog should always look away first. If your puppy has a habit of not breaking eye contact with you, begin training and behavior modification immediately and consider hiring a professional trainer. If you don't know how to handle an assertive dog, your training process can stall or even backfire, leading to worse forms of aggression. A professional trainer will know how to work with your puppy and teach you how to confidently do the same.

Eye blinking is a form of submission. If you look directly into your puppy's eyes and he blinks, it means that he is showing submission and acceptance. Staring and then looking away is also a form of acceptance. The stare might show some desire to be assertive or merely searching for a cue, but breaking off the stare shows that your puppy isn't in the mindset to challenge you at that time.

A dog who looks at you with a soft facial expression, but not directly into your eyes, is a dog who is paying attention to you. He'll blink occasionally, but not constantly. He is relaxed. This dog accepts your leadership and will thus accept your guidance.

Mouth, Teeth and Voice: The dog's mouth conveys a lot of information. Relaxed lips show a relaxed dog. Raised lips can mean one of two things: aggression or submission, depending on how they are raised. A single lip between the gum and teeth,

Did You Know?

Before you begin training, you'll need the following basic equipment:

◆ a buckle or snap-on collar that is comfortable for your puppy. It shouldn't be too loose or too tight. A good rule is to be able to fit two fingers between the collar and your dog's neck.

◆ a 6-foot leash for basic obedience and a 15- to 20-foot leash for long-distance work

◆ a treat pouch filled with treats or your puppy's favorite toy

◆ a clicker or squeaky toy

A dog will tell you a lot with his eyes. Direct eye contact displays dominance, while a puppy who blinks or breaks his gaze when you look at him is showing submission and acceptance.

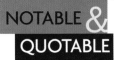

NOTABLE & QUOTABLE

A dog who doesn't understand the basics has little if any means of positive communication with her owner. How can the more complex behavioral challenges be addressed if your dog doesn't even know how to sit on cue?

— *Victoria Schade, a certified pet dog trainer in Annandale, Va.*

CANINE SOCIAL ORDER

Dog and human companionship reflects basic similarities in social structure. We tend to live in groups. We hunt together using strategy. We raise our young together. Some of us are dominant; some are submissive. Some of us are assertive; some are complacent. Some of us are adventurous and active; some are couch potatoes. These attributes make a cohesive society.

Once humans evolved beyond the hunter-gatherer stage, we developed a more complex society, but our basic instincts still exist. Dominant, ambitious and outspoken individuals still control the pack.

Dogs, however, maintained a simple pack social order. They never developed religion, higher education or class structures. Order in a dog pack follows a basic rule: The strongest, most dominant animal is in charge, and the rest form the remainder of the pecking order. Dominance is often fluid within the dog pack. At times, one dog might show dominance over another, then vice versa, depending on the situation. For example, one might be more territorial than the other, initiating the alert, while the other is more possessive of food and will tend to guard the food source more readily.

In dealing with your dog, you must assert yourself as the leader. Dogs rarely understand the human concept of equality. A weakness in his human companion is a gap that must be filled by the canine. If you don't watch over the house, your puppy will. If you allow your dog to sleep on "the throne" (your bed), *you* will be sleeping on the floor, literally and figuratively. If you allow your dog to drag you down the street, he will try to take charge of the whole neighborhood. Kings always seek to rule more territory.

There's an old saying that aptly pertains to the canine–human relationship: "If you win the battle, you win the war." In this case, the battle refers to your behavioral guidelines: what you will and won't allow your puppy to do with you, your family and your home. The war is the overall outcome. Controlled battles will ensure that your puppy turns out to be a great family companion who behaves, listens and is enjoyable.

The word "battle" might have negative connotations, but the analogy is helpful in understanding your responsibilities toward your puppy. You must be clear, consistent and persistent, and you must offer great rewards to ensure a positive outcome.

You must never allow your puppy to do things his way or in his own time. You are the boss; your puppy follows your rules. Dogs need this discipline or they get out of control. You must back up every cue regardless of where you are, what is going on around you and how your puppy reacts. Even a mere slip in allowing your dog to get away with not listening to you can begin the process of your dog's challenging you

Did You Know?

Positive experience is the key to building confidence. The more your pup safely discovers the world, the more confidence and social skills she'll develop. A well-socialized puppy is calmer and behaves more appropriately. She's more able to respond when asked to do things because she doesn't feel worried by nearby events. A well-socialized puppy also tends to be easier to train because she isn't overly distracted and can focus on lessons.

A dog will tell you a lot with his eyes. Direct eye contact displays dominance, while a puppy who blinks or breaks his gaze when you look at him is showing submission and acceptance.

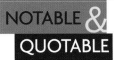

NOTABLE & QUOTABLE

A dog who doesn't understand the basics has little if any means of positive communication with her owner. How can the more complex behavioral challenges be addressed if your dog doesn't even know how to sit on cue?

— *Victoria Schade, a certified pet dog trainer in Annandale, Va.*

showing just the tip of the incisor, can be a sign of insecurity or happiness. The rest of the body will disclose the full message. The lips raised in front, showing the front teeth only, is a sign of submission or fear, depending on other visual cues. For example, a dog who is prancing around while showing his front teeth is expressing a submissive greeting; a dog who is crouching while showing his front teeth is frightened or intimidated.

A dog whose lips are raised enough to show all of the teeth, front to back, is expressing aggression, especially if he is also growling in a low tone. The vocal tone has a lot to do with the meanings of the dog's expressions. A high tone is happy. A medium tone, such as a loud bark, is demanding. A low tone, such as a growl, is aggressive.

Body: A dog who is dominant will try to make himself look large. He'll be raised high on his toes, his head held high, his tail pointed straight out and partly upward, the fur along his spine raised.

A relaxed dog will remain in a normal stance. His tail will be held low (or relaxed into position, if it's a dog with a tail that curls over his back). His ears might swivel from side to side but not perk forward.

A dog who is concentrating and/or working will have a grin on his face. Yes, it's an actual smile, often seen while a dog is enjoying his training time. He'll prance, his tail will wag slowly and his eyes will watch with a cheerful expression.

A dog who is inviting you to play will lower his front end with his hind end in the air, tail wagging. Some dogs will bark, demanding your participation in the game. Many people mistake this for aggression, especially if the dog nips at the person, but this is canine play in its purest form.

When a dog's mouth is relaxed, it shows that he is in a calm state of mind. You can tell more by watching the rest of his body for nonverbal mood indications.

Personality Tests

Here are a few tests to use to discover more about your dog's personality and her future ability to learn using positive reinforcement.

Attentiveness: If your dog likes to lick you, touch you and follow you around, she's a sure thing. If your dog likes to sleep in a room away from you, comes to you for touch only when she feels like it, but does come to you when you call her, she's still a good candidate. If she doesn't listen at all and moves away from you, you most likely won't be able to use positive reinforcement alone; you might also need the aid of a training tool.

Work drive: Most dogs have some sort of prey drive. They'll run after, or at least look at, moving objects. They enjoy their meals and like to go for walks. A dog who will perform well with positive-reinforcement training also has a good work drive.

A dog who is interested in both her environment and where you are in relation to her is a good candidate for positive-reinforcement training. A dog who would rather go after moving critters and objects can still be a good candidate, but you might need to use a training tool to control her when she is distracted.

A dog who doesn't care where you are, doesn't care what you are doing and/or is aggressive will need to be trained with a training tool. If your dog displays any of these traits, consult a professional trainer.

Proceeding with training: For the dog who is responsive and attentive and who has good drive, begin with her as you would a teenage dog or puppy. She'll respond quickly. When she is successful in an area without distractions, gradually add to the distraction level until she is proficient under any circumstances.

For the dog who is still easily distracted, overfriendly with newcomers, or just plain boisterous, use a training device when needed.

For the dog who is more assertive and doesn't care about food, touch and praise rewards, you'll need to begin using a training tool, such as a head halter. Reward her with praise and touch at the very moment she is behaving, even if it is only for a fraction of a second. Breaking the exercises down into minuscule parts will offer frequent rewards, thereby increasing the dog's work drive. As her work drive increases, her inappropriate behavior will gradually subside.

CANINE SOCIAL ORDER

Dog and human companionship reflects basic similarities in social structure. We tend to live in groups. We hunt together using strategy. We raise our young together. Some of us are dominant; some are submissive. Some of us are assertive; some are complacent. Some of us are adventurous and active; some are couch potatoes. These attributes make a cohesive society.

Once humans evolved beyond the hunter-gatherer stage, we developed a more complex society, but our basic instincts still exist. Dominant, ambitious and outspoken individuals still control the pack.

Dogs, however, maintained a simple pack social order. They never developed religion, higher education or class structures. Order in a dog pack follows a basic rule: The strongest, most dominant animal is in charge, and the rest form the remainder of the pecking order. Dominance is often fluid within the dog pack. At times, one dog might show dominance over another, then vice versa, depending on the situation. For example, one might be more territorial than the other, initiating the alert, while the other is more possessive of food and will tend to guard the food source more readily.

In dealing with your dog, you must assert yourself as the leader. Dogs rarely understand the human concept of equality. A weakness in his human companion is a gap that must be filled by the canine. If you don't watch over the house, your puppy will. If you allow your dog to sleep on "the throne" (your bed), *you* will be sleeping on the floor, literally and figuratively. If you allow your dog to drag you down the street, he will try to take charge of the whole neighborhood. Kings always seek to rule more territory.

There's an old saying that aptly pertains to the canine–human relationship: "If you win the battle, you win the war." In this case, the battle refers to your behavioral guidelines: what you will and won't allow your puppy to do with you, your family and your home. The war is the overall outcome. Controlled battles will ensure that your puppy turns out to be a great family companion who behaves, listens and is enjoyable.

The word "battle" might have negative connotations, but the analogy is helpful in understanding your responsibilities toward your puppy. You must be clear, consistent and persistent, and you must offer great rewards to ensure a positive outcome.

You must never allow your puppy to do things his way or in his own time. You are the boss; your puppy follows your rules. Dogs need this discipline or they get out of control. You must back up every cue regardless of where you are, what is going on around you and how your puppy reacts. Even a mere slip in allowing your dog to get away with not listening to you can begin the process of your dog's challenging you

Did You Know?

Positive experience is the key to building confidence. The more your pup safely discovers the world, the more confidence and social skills she'll develop. A well-socialized puppy is calmer and behaves more appropriately. She's more able to respond when asked to do things because she doesn't feel worried by nearby events. A well-socialized puppy also tends to be easier to train because she isn't overly distracted and can focus on lessons.

Move slowly when interacting with a fearful or dominant puppy. Give the dog space if he appears to be territorial; let him come to you.

for leadership. If you make your dog earn all of his rewards — food and attention of any sort — you will have a dog who is always looking for ways to perform for you instead of a dog who demands your performance for him.

Another saying that can be applied to dogs is, "Give him an inch, and he'll take a mile." A concession may be nearly imperceptible to you, but not to your dog. Once your dog thinks he has won an inch, he will start to take more of them. Once your puppy recognizes your breaking point, he will strive to reach it in every challenge. If you show him that you have no breaking point and that you will persist until he does as you wish, you will find him complying faster and faster. If you assume your leadership responsibilities starting with your first day of dog ownership, there will be very few "battles" to deal with; you'll merely have minor challenges as your dog goes through his behavioral development.

it's a Fact

There are two types of submissive behavior: active and passive. An actively submissive dog is the type that might fear bite if she is cornered and sees no way out of the situation. This dog will hold her body low to the ground, hackles raised, neck stretched out and teeth bared. Her tail will be between her legs. Never approach a dog who shows these behaviors. Some do not growl to warn; they simply lash out. Take the time to allow the dog to come to you. Do not reach out to pet her. Let her sniff you first. Every step must be taken very slowly and methodically. Allow the dog to make the first moves.

A passively submissive dog will try to make herself as small as possible. She will tuck her tail under her body, lower her head, and possibly roll over onto her back, showing you her belly. Some dogs will urinate. Submissive urination should never be misconstrued as a housetraining problem, and the dog should never be punished for this type of accident. She is simply showing you that you are the leader and that she defers to you in that uncontested position.

SOLUTIONS

Dogs learn from their owners and from each other. This is a natural aspect of social life. Puppies learn from adults, just as children learn from parents and teachers. Your new dog will be looking to you to learn how to behave in his new home and with his new family.

Before you start developing a training schedule, though, you must keep in mind that puppies are social creatures. Each puppy needs to be immersed in his environment, have plenty of opportunities to interact with that environment and decide that his new environment is a great place to be.

ENVIRONMENT IMMERSION

Dogs learn from their peers. In puppyhood, dogs learn a lot about how to socialize with other canines, which prepares them to interact with their future human packs. Without this early education, your puppy may have behavioral issues as he matures — issues such as aggression toward dogs, possessive aggression and a general lack of social graces.

Besides socializing your puppy with his new family, you should also expose him to other people, animals and situations. However, he must not come

it's a Fact Small dogs enjoy squeaky toys, small nylon bones, stuffed toys and rubber toys. Always buy toys that are made for the breed size that you own.

into close contact with dogs you don't know well until after he has had all of his vaccinations. Introducing him to new people and surroundings will make him more well adjusted. As he grows up he'll be less prone to timid or fearful behavior when he encounters new things.

Your pup's socialization began wherever he lived before you adopted him — whether at the breeder's home, a shelter or elsewhere. But now it is your responsibility to continue the interaction. The socialization he receives up to 12 weeks old is the most critical, as this is the time when he forms his impressions of the outside world. Be especially careful during the eight- to 10-week period, also known as the "fear" period. The interaction he receives during this time should be gentle and reassuring. Lack of socialization can manifest itself as fear and aggression as a dog grows up. A pup needs a lot of human contact, affection, handling and exposure to other animals.

Once your puppy has received his necessary vaccinations, feel free to take him out and about (on leash, of course). Walk him around the neighborhood, take him on your daily errands, let people pet him, let him meet other dogs and pets. Make sure to expose your puppy to different people: men, women, children, babies, men with beards, teenagers talking on cell phones or riding skateboards, joggers, shoppers, people in wheelchairs, pregnant women, etc. Make sure your puppy explores different surfaces like sidewalks, gravel and puddles. Positive experiences are the key to building confidence. It's up to you to make sure your puppy safely discovers the world so that he grows into a calm, confident and well-socialized adult.

It's important that you take the

If socialized properly, puppies and cats can become lifelong friends.

Some ordinary household items make great toys for your puppy — as long as they are safe. Tennis balls, plastic water bottles, old towels and more can be transformed into fun toys with a little creativity. You will find a list of homemade toys at **Dog Channel.com/Club-Pup** — just click on "downloads."

JOIN OUR ONLINE
Club
Pup™

Socialization to a number of experiences is key for young puppies to prepare them for the rest of their lives.

Always introduce your pup to things safely so she will build confidence.

Did You Know?

Playing with your dog is more than just fun and games. Play reduces stress, provides aerobic exercise, improves motor skills and decreases the incidence of behavioral problems, such as chewing, barking and digging. It enhances social interactions with other dogs, and, perhaps most importantly, it strengthens the human-canine bond.

lead in all socialization experiences and never put your pup in scary or potentially harmful situations. Be mindful of your puppy's limitations. Fifteen minutes at a public market is fine; two hours at a loud outdoor concert is too much. Meeting vaccinated, tolerant and gentle older dogs is great. Meeting dogs you don't know isn't a great idea, especially if they appear very energetic, dominant or fearful.

The best way to socialize your puppy to a new experience is to make him think it's the best thing ever. You can do this using a lot of happy talk, enthusiasm, and, of course, food. To convince your puppy that

JOIN OUR ONLINE Club Pup™

A great way to reward your puppy for a job well done is to provide her with bite-sized treats. You can purchase all sorts of treats from a pet-supply store, and you can even make your own. Go online to download a treat recipe at **DogChannel.com/Club-Pup**

SMART TIP!

Puppies love to play and romp, and they let you — and other dogs — know that they want to play through unmistakable body language and verbalizations. Perhaps the best-recognized dog gesture is the play bow: forelegs flat on the ground, rear end high in the air, mouth wide open, tail wagging wildly. Try giving a play bow back to your dog. She'll get even more excited and may follow up with playful attacks and retreats.

almost any experience is a blast, always carry treats. Consider carrying two types: a bag of his puppy chow so you can give him pieces while introducing him to nonthreatening experiences and a bag of high-value, mouth-watering treats for introducing him to less familiar experiences.

ENVIRONMENTAL INTERACTION

All dogs need physical stimulation, but different breeds require different amounts of exercise. Be sure to research your dog's breed to learn exactly how much and what type of activity he requires. For example, Border Collies are a herding breed and are high-energy dogs; they require hours of exercise every day. Mastiffs, on the other hand, are guard dogs and are more accustomed to remaining in one place; they require just a couple of mild workouts each day. Your puppy's age will also play a role in his exercise requirements. Puppies between the ages of 2 and 4 months old need short, frequent exercise sessions. Older puppies require longer, more frequent sessions, and adult dogs require one or two exercise sessions per day. The more exercise your puppy gets, the easier he will be to live with.

Even when your puppy becomes an adult, he will want to spend time playing with other dogs. His human family members just can't fill this role. I doubt you'd want to roll around on the ground with him, grab his tail or run around fetching a stick. Humans just aren't built for that type of play. Dogs need this canine interaction for physical and mental health.

If you can't find any neighborhood playmates for your puppy, consider getting a second dog, especially if you work long hours and your puppy spends a lot of time home alone each day. Having a canine companion will help him receive appropriate social time and exercise, and it will relieve his loneliness. Another option is doggie day care. This will minimize the chance of separation anxiety, and it will help your puppy learn to properly socialize with a variety of canine personalities.

Your dog also needs mental stimulation from toys, games and training. Keeping your puppy busy will curb destructive behavior. Offer him at least six different toys at a time. A large dog, for example, would enjoy an assortment of appropriately-sized hard-rubber toys, hard-nylon chew bones and dental bones.

A word of advice about rawhide: Only let your puppy have large bones. When a rawhide bone is chewed down to a small size or if he tears off a piece, throw it away. Little pieces of rawhide can easily lodge in the roof of a dog's mouth or in his throat, causing him to choke. Furthermore, rawhide is not digestible. Too much ingested rawhide can cause vomiting or diarrhea. If you're going to buy rawhide, keep it as a special once-in-a-while treat. Edible and digestible hard bones made of vegetable matter are now available, and

Separation Anxiety

What is commonly called "separation anxiety" in dogs is expressed by whining, barking or destructive behavior that takes place after the owner departs. Unfortunately, much of this anxiety is actually caused by the owner. If you make a big production of leaving, your puppy will go right into her canine con-game with whines and barks that you translate into, "Please don't leave me! Please take me with you!" And so on. As long as you keep up your end of the conversation, she's got you!

Preventing separation anxiety is simple, so start off on the right foot. When you are ready to leave the house, put your dog in her approved area (like a crate or X-pen) with water, toys and perhaps a dog biscuit. Put on your hat and coat, pick up your car keys, give her a simple, "Bye! See you later" and leave. That's it. When you return, don't make an exuberant fuss over your pup as you walk through the door. Put down your purse or briefcase and take off your coat while telling her how pleased you are that she took your phone messages. After a calm entry, you can then give in to the all-out petting, cuddling or whatever!

We mentioned previously about the "fear phase" that puppies can go through, but face it: If your dog doesn't get along well with strange people or other dogs, keeping her away from the situations will only make it worse. Let friends and relatives come over to meet the new addition to your family. Arm them with tiny treats to hold in their outstretched palms if the pup shows any signs of shyness. (Whole-grain cereals work great!)

Puppy kindergarten classes are good for encouraging pups to become well-socialized dogs. You'll learn a lot, too, as you and your puppy will be part of a group of other pups and their owners. These classes are primarily to establish social manners among the puppies, and therefore obedience comes into play. So, it's a good all-around education.

Physical and mental stimulation can come from toys or other dogs.

they might be a better alternative to rawhide. Most puppies enjoy them as much as they like rawhide bones. But still keep an eye out for loose stool or vomiting, as some dogs have trouble digesting these substances as well.

The best way to keep your puppy mentally stimulated is to train him and teach him to do tricks. Dogs love learning, especially if it involves getting special rewards and praise in the process. Don't wait until your puppy acclimates fully to his new home to start teaching him. He'll settle in much faster if you begin training him right away. Puppies as young as 8 weeks old are able to comprehend and respond to cues. In fact, when you train a puppy, you're essentially starting with a clean slate and a mind that soaks up instruction like a sponge. If you postpone training until your puppy gets older, you'll have to contend with breaking bad habits, overcoming behavioral problems and facing a resistant adolescent's personality.

Dogs who play regularly with other dogs have fewer fear and aggression problems with other dogs, as well as fewer behavior problems related to lack of stimulation, such as chewing, digging and barking. — Jean Donaldson, director of the Academy for Dog Trainers at the San Francisco Society for the Prevention of Cruelty to Animals

Food is a great motivator for training sessions, but keep the portions small to keep your puppy engaged.

SMART TIP!

To maintain your puppy's interest in her toys, rotate them daily. Present her with three on one day and a different three on the next. Every day, her reaction will be, "Oh boy! A new toy!" This is much better than her deciding that your leather loafers or coffee-table legs might be fun to play with.

Even if your pup is older than 6 months of age when you get him, bringing him into his new home is a great opportunity to begin teaching him about what is and is not allowed in his environment. Start your puppy on the right track, and he'll never let you down.

LOVING THE ENVIRONMENT

Positive reinforcement is the most effective and humane training method currently in use. The method teaches that you train your puppy to behave by rewarding him for his behavior every time he does something you want him to do. To reach the ultimate goal — teaching your puppy a specific behavior — you will need to break each behavior down into smaller, more easily achievable goals. This will encourage your dog to learn at an accelerated pace with a great attitude, as he's rewarded for small successes along the way.

For your puppy to want to learn, he first has to be presented with his reward without actually thinking that he is being forced into anything. This reward is called a "lure." A lure can be a tasty treat or a favorite toy. Using the lure, you can guide a dog into any position or response without the dog knowing the meaning of your cue. By pairing the cue with the action, through repetition, your puppy will learn the meaning of the word and eventually respond to it without seeing the lure directly in front of him. Instead, he will perform for the promise of his reward.

To reduce the use of a lure, you'll need a way to let your puppy know that he will eventually receive his reward. This is called a bridge. A bridging signal can be verbal praise or a specific noise, such as a squeaky toy or a clicker. By pairing the bridging signal with the reward, the dog will learn that they both have the same meaning: It's payday.

To begin teaching your puppy that the bridging signal means payday, you'll first need to associate it with his reward. For explanation purposes, we'll use the clicker as our bridging signal. Clicker training is a popular positive-reinforcement training method that utilizes a small, plastic hand-held clicker to bridge the cue and your puppy's reward.

If you wish to clicker train at this point, you'll need to begin with "charging your clicker." This means teaching your puppy to connect the sound of the clicker with receiving a reward. He should have the idea after three to five tries.

To start the process, show your puppy his treat, then click and praise as you give him his treat. Repeat this three to five times until he learns.

Next, put the treat inside your fist and show your closed fist to your puppy. When he touches your fist, sniffing for the treat, click and open your fist; then give him his treat. Repeat this three times.

Your puppy now knows how to "target." When you present your fist and he touches it, you will click and praise and he will get

his reward. Targeting is the basis for every training technique that will follow.

You can test your puppy's targeting abilities by moving your hand left or right, up or down. His head will follow your hand. As it does, click, praise and reward. Gradually ask for more movement each time you hold out your hand. This is forming a behavior chain. Your puppy has to do more to earn his treat.

At any time during this targeting, did you say anything other than, "Good dog"? No. Yet, your pup did learn to target. He also learned that a click and praise means that good things are on the way. In essence, he taught himself by associating your hand cue with the bridge and reward — and he loves it!

Now you have the idea. Your puppy is lured into position. As soon as he attains the desired position, bridge (click) and reward.

WALKING

Teaching your puppy to walk on a loose leash is probably one of the more difficult behaviors to teach. Most people have a habit of holding the leash tightly or pulling back whenever their dog pulls away, which only makes the dog pull harder. Constant tension on the leash will teach a dog to keep pulling. It's a natural reaction.

The instinctual tendency to pull might be more developed in the working breeds, but it is intrinsic in all breeds. The Siberian Husky, Alaskan Malamute and Samoyed are specifically bred to pull sleds and thus have stronger instincts to pull. But a little Pomeranian can do the same, especially considering that he is descended from the aforementioned Nordic breeds. A Yorkshire Terrier will pull, as will a Cocker Spaniel. If you apply pressure, any dog will return it.

Did You Know?

Identification for your puppy is like insurance: Hopefully, you'll never need it, but if you do, you'll be glad it's there. The most traditional form of ID is a collar with tags: quick, easy and inexpensive. You can purchase a metal or plastic tag imprinted with information (your name, address and phone number) and attach it to your puppy's collar. Tattoos and microchips are also good ways to ID your puppy and are less easy to wiggle out of.

Teach your puppy to heel and walk on a loose leash, and she'll be a much more enjoyable — and safer — travel companion.

The key to teaching your dog not to pull on the leash is to avoid applying any pressure. How do you do that, you ask? How do you not pull back when your dog is dragging you down the sidewalk at warp speed? You teach him how to pay attention and how much more fulfilling it is to walk at your side than to run to the end of the leash,

it's a Fact

Training works best when incorporated into daily life. When your puppy asks for something — food, play, whatever— cue her to do something for you first. Reward her by granting her request. Practice in different settings, so your puppy learns to listen regardless of her surroundings.

straining and choking. You have to offer a better alternative; you have to condition your puppy to prefer the correct action.

The method you use to train your puppy to heel depends largely on his age. It also depends on your ultimate goals. Do you want him to perform in obedience trials or to just walk with you around the neighborhood? You have to define your goals prior to starting your training. Communicate to your dog when you want him to pay attention and when he's allowed to sniff and investigate. Your puppy will need to listen regardless of where he is and what is going on around him, and he'll need to do so on one cue. Set your parameters, and stick to them.

Once you have set your goals, you'll need to plan your behavior-shaping routine. Remember that you must stay a step or two ahead of your dog. If he accomplishes several steps very quickly, move on to the next step. If he seems to lose the

With enough repetition, your puppy will learn to associate certain words you say with certain actions he does. Eventually, he'll understand that "Let's go for a walk" means it's time to explore the great outdoors.

Did You Know?

Learning comes simply and naturally when you teach puppies to associate certain words and behaviors. That's where talking to them and spending lots of time with them comes in. Dogs are capable of learning an extensive vocabulary, simply by watching and listening to you. For instance, your puppy will learn quickly that when you put on a certain pair of shoes, it's time for a walk. The pup is primed to respond to you, so teach a phrase to go along with the action, such as "Let's go for a walk" or "Let's go for a car ride."

SMART TIP!

Venturing outside the security of the house and yard can be exciting — and scary — for both you and your puppy. Here's how to make your time together away from home more fun than fearsome.

- Keep your puppy on a leash at all times.
- Avoid areas where nonimmunized dogs congregate, until your puppy has received all of her vaccinations.
- Avoid areas where dogs run loose, including dog parks.
- Watch for potential hazards, such as traffic, people (adults and children), dogs and other animals.

ability to perform at a specific level, go back a step or two to a level at which he responds properly and move forward again. There is no fixed timetable for accomplishing any single behavior, only a means of gradually shaping a response into your ultimate goal.

Be flexible.
Be consistent.
Be persistent.
Be patient.

Be generous with your praise, and always keep the training fun and positive.

TRAINING A PUPPY

Puppies may have short attention spans, but they are quick and eager learners. They are very attached to their pack members and tend to remain close by, which makes teaching attentiveness relatively easy. The younger the pup, the easier it is to gain his attention. As the pup gets older, 3 months old or more, distractions in his environment may take precedence if you haven't taught him that being attentive is more rewarding.

At this stage, you don't want to work with the leash. Yes, we are starting this training off leash before attempting it on leash. This will allow you to concentrate on attaining the appropriate response from your pup without having to fiddle with the leash as well. Once the puppy has an idea of what to do, add the leash.

Puppies tend to have a high food drive; therefore, they respond well to food rewards and quickly learn that the bridging sound (clicker or squeaker) is associated with food.

Initial training sessions should take place in a familiar setting. Make sure that he has already explored the surroundings and that there are no new distractions. A small room or a quiet yard is ideal.

Begin by teaching your puppy to target. Hold a treat in one hand; make certain it's in your left hand if you want him to walk on your left side and in your right hand if you want him to walk on your right side. Put the treat under his nose to gain his attention. As soon as you have it, click, praise and give the treat. Move the target slightly to one side. As your puppy follows, praise and give him the treat. Move the target slightly to the other side. Again, as your puppy follows with his nose, praise and give him the treat. Repeat with a slight up-and-down motion. As he follows your hand, praise and then click and reward. You now have the puppy targeting. In the few minutes it took to teach your puppy to target, he learned a couple of new behaviors: the meaning of your bridge and praise, as well as the concept that following his nose brings great rewards.

Give your puppy a break for a couple minutes. You'll need to identify this relaxation

Puppies are social creatures. Some assert their dominance as leaders of their packs, while others submit. The key is to train your dog to submit to you as his pack leader.

time in some manner, so begin each break by saying a specific word such as "break," "release" or "free time," making sure to always use the same word. As soon as you utter the relaxation cue, pet your pup. The action of petting distracts him from the targeting routine because dogs love being touched. It's a great reward and is a positive means of ending your training sessions.

Once you have your puppy's attention focused on the appropriate hand, place that hand near your calf. As your puppy follows your hand, praise and reward him when he touches it with his nose. He should do so fairly quickly. If not, lure him there by allowing him to sniff your hand and then slowly bringing your hand to your lower leg.

If your pup doesn't seem to be interested in the treat, you may need to try something else to get his attention. Remember one of the first things you should do, prior to training, is discover what "drives" your puppy.

it's a Fact

Pet dogs, though domesticated, interact with each other according to pack protocol. The pack (the basic canine social unit) is structured around a hierarchy of dominance and subordinates (submission). Every pack member is dominant to some and subordinate to others, with the exception of the alpha (who is dominant over all) and the lowest-ranking pack member (who is subordinate to all). Social rank is communicated and enforced through body language — a complex combination of movements, posture and other physical signals.

What food will he go crazy over? What toy will he do anything to get? Use a valuable motivator. If your puppy wants the reward, he'll do whatever it takes to get it and will learn at an accelerated rate.

When you have your puppy's attention at your leg, take one step forward, using the leg that he is targeting, and give the cue you wish to use for the exercise, such as "walk," "heel" or "let's go." As he moves with you, following his target, praise, stop, and then bridge and reward.

The next level is taking two steps as your puppy follows your target. Praise, bridge and reward as he remains at your side for two steps. Each successful time you tell your puppy to heel, add another step. Within a few minutes, you'll be walking eight to 10 steps, or more!

Give your puppy a break for a few minutes and then repeat the exercise, starting at five steps and working up to 15. Take another rest period and begin at 10 steps, shaping your way up to 20.

Once your puppy is heeling nicely, begin incorporating turns. Step forward about five steps, turn right, stop, praise, click and reward. Repeat at least three times. Then go forward a variable amount of steps, turn, stop, praise, click and reward. The next time, add a few steps beyond the turn prior to bridging. Then do the same with a left turn. Start to vary the directions of your turns and the number of steps before and after each turn. Be sure to give your pup a break every three to five minutes. If he starts to show signs of disinterest — for example, if he sniffs at the ground, looks away, or lags — stop. Always end on a good note, with your puppy performing an exercise correctly.

As your puppy starts to pick up the routine, you can begin reducing the baiting/luring procedures. Gradually lift the target higher and start to straighten yourself out. (You can only stay hunched over for so long.) Provided your puppy maintains the proper trajectory (remaining in the heel position), praise, click and reward upon stopping. Don't give him the food reward as often; instead, praise to reinforce his correct behavior.

TRAINING THE ADOLESCENT DOG

If your dog isn't really a puppy (younger than 4 months of age) but isn't quite an adult yet (up to 2 or 3 years of age, depending on the breed), you'll have to approach heel training from a different angle.

This is probably the most challenging age to train dogs, as they are in the process of establishing their place within the family, and they are easily distracted and full of energy. Adolescent dogs are no longer glued to pack members; they'd rather be out and about, exploring new territory and testing their potential.

You can try starting out with the same procedures you'd use with a young pup, but they won't work when your dog is exposed to any distractions. They also won't work if your dog is being assertive. In fact, it will be difficult to use purely positive reinforcement at this time. You will need to use other training tools to redirect his attention back to you. The tools most recommended are head halters and front-connecting harnesses. If your dog is very strong, he might require a head halter. If your dog is a small dog or doesn't typically pull on his leash, then a front-connecting harness will be sufficient.

To be sure that your adolescent dog starts to get the idea, begin by working with him in a quiet area without distractions. Use a reward that he'll go bonkers over; it must have a high value to maintain his attention.

JOIN OUR
ONLINE
Club
Pup™

With the proper training, your puppy will be as well behaved as she is adorable. One certification that all dogs should receive is the American Kennel Club Canine Good Citizen, which rewards dogs with good manners. Go to **DogChannel.com/Club-Pup** and click on "Downloads" to get the 10 steps required for your dog to be a CGC.

Some trainers have had success with freeze-dried liver, small slices of hot dog or bits of cheese. Make sure that whatever you use won't upset your puppy's digestive system. These high-value treats are very rich foods, and a dog with a sensitive stomach can have a bad reaction to them. In this case, venison or lamb can be a great treat without causing stomach upset.

Once you've charged your clicker, you can now shape the heel position. When your dog looks at you, praise, then click and give the reward by either tossing the treat to your dog or having him come to you to get it. If you are using a lure, show him the reward and allow him to come for it. As he does so, praise, then click and reward. When he takes a step toward you, praise, click and reward. After he takes two steps toward you, praise, click and reward. Continue until he is near you.

Turn so that your dog is at your side. As soon as he's in the correct position, even if you have to put yourself in the position, praise, click and reward. If he remains in position, praise again, click and reward. As he remains, click and reward. If he moves, don't do anything; just wait. When he puts himself into the heel position, praise, click and reward. If he fails to put himself into the heel position, lure him there with the bait and then praise, click and reward.

Now add the heel cue. Say his name and then the cue. Do this only one time. Never repeat your cue; repetition just becomes background noise that your dog learns to ignore. The cue has no meaning if you don't associate it with the response you expect when you say it. Give the cue as your puppy places himself or maintains the heel position.

Holding the reward on your leg, just out of his reach, is another great means of

explaining what you want. The lure will put him into position without you physically having to do so, and it's faster than just waiting for the behavior to occur. As soon as your puppy puts himself into position, praise, click and reward. Continue to do so as he remains in position.

Take a step forward as you say your dog's name, then "heel." Lure with the food. As he remains in the heel position at your side, praise, click and reward. If he doesn't remain in position, lure him back with the bait. Always praise, click and reward when your puppy attains the position you requested.

Once you are able to take more than a couple of steps and your puppy remains at your side, praise him while he maintains his place. Click and reward when you stop,

Begin training your puppy to heel without a leash in a familiar room with no new distractions. Heeling can be difficult to master but is an invaluable obedience tool.

NOTABLE & QUOTABLE

I put no pressure on the leash [when training the heel cue]. In my hand, I hold a hot dog or a toy at my thigh, where heel position is, and say, "Puppy, heel." Off we go, even if it's just 10 steps. I keep my right wrist at my thigh so the toy or hot dog is right where the puppy's nose is. After three weeks of that, they know where the heel position is, and if they're not there, they correct themselves.

— Rottweiler breeder Paula Cingota of Jamul, Calif.

SMART TIP!

If you begin teaching the heel cue by taking long walks and letting your dog pull you along, she may misinterpret this action as acceptable. When you pull back on the leash to counteract her pulling, she will read that tug as a signal to pull even harder!

signaling the end of the exercise. This does not necessarily mean a release time or break, just the end of that heeling moment. After his reward, you can give him the cue again and continue. In fact, unless you are planning to let him take a break, go directly into the heel again. Waiting a few seconds will only give your puppy a chance to be distracted from the exercise, which means you'll have to start over again. This can be frustrating for you both.

Gradually shape your puppy into a heeling machine. Turn a couple of steps into three, four and so on until you can move forward 20 steps or more, turn left and right, and vary your pace. Give him a break every five minutes or so, and pet or play with him. This way, you are ending the exercise with something positive.

Now it's time to work around distractions. Most adolescent dogs will try to pull away, want to sniff interesting scents and enjoy jumping around. They are teenagers. They have lots of energy. Allow your dog to let off some steam prior to training. Play fetch or race around an enclosed area with him — anything to take the edge off. Your puppy can't concentrate if he doesn't receive enough exercise.

When confronted with distractions, many adolescent dogs couldn't care less about food or toys. They'd rather investigate, race after or otherwise engage the distraction. Without a means of redirection (such as a collar or halter), you don't stand a chance of regaining his attention.

Be patient, and positive-reinforcement training will work. Give your cue once, then wait for your puppy to assume the correct stance before you praise and reward the behavior.

A well-behaved dog begins with a well-trained puppy.

SIT, DOWN

To bring out the best in your puppy, teach him with a positive training method as discussed earlier. Start when he's young — as soon as you bring him home. Waiting until he's 6 months old is a serious waste of good training time; at that age, he'll be much larger, more difficult to control and more easily distracted.

To get started, all puppies, regardless of your training and relationship goals, need to know at least the basic good-manner behaviors: sit, down and stay. Don't worry. It's easier to train these basic cues than you think.

THE SIT CUE

The easiest way to get started with the sit cue is to use a food lure. Once your dog is lured into position, you can praise, click and reward. Sounds easy, right? It should be, but, then again, dogs aren't robots. Dogs are as unique as individual humans are. Each dog will respond to cues differently. Not all dogs are driven by food rewards. Some prefer touch, verbal praise or special toys. Others don't care about any positive reinforcement.

Luring with Food: Most dogs follow their noses. To lure your puppy into position, you only need to put a treat — such as a training treat, a piece of kibble, etc. — in the right spot and then praise, click and treat as soon as he attains the desired position. The tricky part is knowing where to place the treat.

When luring your puppy to sit, you'll want to place your lure directly between and slightly above his eyes, just a few inches out of reach. He'll try to reach the food by looking upward. As he looks upward, his rear end will lower. As this happens — even just a little — praise, click and give him his treat.

If your puppy doesn't do a full sit on the first try, that's OK. Repeat the exercise and request just a little more each time. If your puppy tries jumping up to get his treat, you're holding it too high above his head, it should be just a few inches above his eyes.

Some dogs may need a helping hand because they are so excited about the exercise that they just can't sit still. To aid an overanxious puppy, gently press his bottom as you lure his nose upward. Praise, click and reward the second that his rump touches down. You may need to assist him a few times, but he'll catch on.

Add the sit cue, say your pup's name and "sit," as you place your lure over his head and between his eyes. Follow up with saying "good dog" as he attains the position while you click and give him the treat.

Luring with a Toy: This process is pretty much the same as luring with food. The difference is that you'll have to release your puppy after each successful exercise because he'll want to play with his toy. Without this

Did You Know?

Puppies tend to perform best when you work in short time spans. For example, either ask for three to five responses and stop, or work for a minute and a half and stop. This will maintain your puppy's attention span for a longer period of time. She will want to continue, deepening her desire to perform.

reinforcement, the toy lure won't work. Gradually, you'll be able to have your puppy do more behaviors with fewer playtime releases. In general, however, it tends to take a little longer to lure puppies to behaviors with toys than with food.

Luring with Touch: Chances are you won't be able to lure your puppy with the promise of touch. There's really no way to let a dog know that you intend to pet him if he'll sit for you. Instead of luring your puppy into position, therefore, you'll have to place him there, using touch, of course. Once he's in position, caress him in a favorite spot, such as his chest or tummy, or rub his ears. After several repetitions,

He can't read a training manual, so it's your job to train your puppy.

your puppy will get the idea that you'll pet him when he's in the sit position, so he'll gladly put himself there.

To pair the use of the clicker with this reward method, you'll probably need an extra hand. It's easier to add the clicker later, when your puppy has a better understanding of the exercise and you don't have to actually place him into position. Another alternative is to use your voice to click. Some people use an enthusiastic "yes" while others imitate the sound of the click or use the word "good." It really won't take too many tries to have your dog sit on cue. Even many of the more assertive personalities will sit for rewards.

USING THE SIT CUE

Once your puppy has an idea of how to sit, you can incorporate the exercise into his behavioral repertoire in many ways. He can sit at your side when you are heeling. He can sit for attention versus jumping up for attention. He can sit when you are examining or bathing him.

To work the sit cue into the heeling routine, do the following:

Step one: Walk with your puppy heeling at your side for a couple of steps. As you stop, show your puppy the treat, hold it just out of his reach between his eyes, and say "sit."

Step two: When your puppy's rump touches down, praise, click and reward.

Step three: Repeat throughout your heeling exercise. Within a short time, your puppy will be sitting automatically when you stop walking.

You have now paired two behaviors. This is called "behavior chaining." Your puppy must do more to attain his bridge and reward. He will also tend to remain closer to your side while heeling because you are maintaining his attention even as you stop.

The basic cues of sit, down and stay are essential for your puppy to learn, and breaking down the cues to their simplest components will make success easy.

To teach your puppy to sit for attention, do the following:

Step one: When he's jumping up on you, move away. Don't give him any positive attention. Merely speaking to him can encourage more jumping.

Step two: Show your puppy the treat. Hold it between his eyes.

Step three: Say "sit." Use a commanding tone of voice. Don't yell or repeat yourself.

Step four: Lure him into the sit position.

Step five: As soon as he attains this position, praise, click and reward.

Step six: Repeat as necessary.

To continually reinforce the sit, you'll need to observe your puppy's behavior closely outside of training sessions. If he just happens to come up to you and sit, reward him with much enthusiasm. If you don't, the behavior you worked so hard to achieve will quickly be extinguished.

THE DOWN CUE

One of the most difficult behaviors to teach is the down cue. You'll understand the difficulty when you realize that the down position represents submission. Dogs instinctively feel very vulnerable in the down position and will naturally assume it only to show subservience to a dominant animal. Lying down on cue is contrary to your puppy's instincts.

> **it's a Fact**
>
> **The basic form of targeting is called luring.** By moving a piece of food in front of a dog's mouth, you can get her to sit, lie down, dance on her hind legs or roll over. This aspect of targeting is as old as domestication.

To succeed at teaching this cue, you have to assume and maintain leadership of your pack. Your puppy won't care a bit about responding to the down cue if he doesn't first respect you. Don't allow yourself to become lenient. You don't have to be mean about it; just be assertive and persistent.

There are different ways to lure your puppy into the down position. You can do it either standing in front of him or from the heel position. Which position to use depends on whether your puppy is easy to lure downward.

From the Front:

● Stand in front of your puppy and request the sit cue.

● As soon as he sits, click, praise and reward.

● Show him your hand with the treat inside and have him target on it, then praise, click and reward.

● Lower your hand directly under his nose. Have your puppy target on it, and praise him as he does.

● Repeat the exercise, gradually lowering your hand with the treat once each time you lower your hand until the target touches the ground. Your puppy will lower his shoulders more each time he targets.

Your goal is to have your puppy lying down, tummy touching the ground. Within a few repetitions, he should do this without you having to touch him. However, as soon as he accomplishes the down behavior, praise, click and reward along with giving him a break from work and a belly rub.

For resistant dogs, use lots of patience. Break the exercise down into small components. Begin with just getting your puppy's head looking down. Once he's accomplished this, don't bridge and reward until he also begins lowering his upper body. Gradually require more and more lowering

Most puppies are eager to learn; use this time to instill good training and obedience habits in your pup that will last a lifetime.

SMART TIP!

Owners who are new to positive training methods that utilize treats often have difficulty down the road in getting their dogs to perform without rewards. You can accomplish this, however, by advancing to a variable reinforcement schedule, whereby you reward randomly. Sometimes you reward a correct performance two times in a row, sometimes you wait until the third repetition, and sometimes you treat the first and fifth times. Occasionally, you should offer a jackpot reward of multiple treats. In short, keep your puppy performing by keeping her guessing.

prior to bridging and offering a reward. Eventually, your puppy will lie completely down, but that will take some time, as he needs to learn that the position isn't negative to him in any manner. At first, don't expect him to remain in position for more than a second or two.

When your puppy has a general understanding of the down cue, repeat the exercise using only a visual cue (hand signal), always using the bridge and rewarding at the appropriate times. Once you've been able to establish a behavior threshold — he remains in position for a couple of seconds before receiving his reward — you'll be able to begin teaching the down/stay (described later in this chapter).

For obstinate dogs who won't go all the way down for treats, lure them into the down position from the heel position.

From the Heel Position:

■ Practice heeling and sitting for a couple of minutes. Always begin with behaviors your puppy knows well and for which you give positive feedback.

■ Have your puppy sit at your side.

■ With your puppy in the heel position, put your target hand directly beneath his nose and allow him to sniff the treat.

■ Lower your hand to the ground as you give the down cue.

If he lowers himself, *bravo*! He learns quickly, and you'll have no need to physically place him into position. If not, continue with the following steps:

● Holding your treat directly under his nose, put some pressure just behind his shoulder blades. If this is enough for your puppy to decide to lower himself, praise, click and reward.

● If this isn't enough to get your dog into the down position, you'll need both hands to place your puppy. Put the leash in your left hand if he is on your left side or in your right hand if he is on your right side and apply pressure just behind his shoulder blades,

● As you apply the pressure, bring his forelegs directly forward while you gently press your puppy into the down position. The easiest way to bring out a big dog's forelegs is to pass your hand behind the leg nearest to you, grasp the far leg and sweep both legs forward. As soon as his belly touches the ground, praise and reward. Go directly into the heel exercise. As he accepts being placed into position, praise and have him remain a second or two longer prior to receiving his reward. This will prepare him for the down/stay.

Your puppy will move downward easier and easier with each successive down exercise. As soon as he does so without you having to place him, you can again pair the click with the verbal praise and reward.

Build on the successes, not the failures. Always reinforce with praise and reward whenever you introduce a new behavior or variation. With each incremental success, increase the criterion. First be successful at one step, then at two, and so on until you reach your goal. Eventually, the only bridge you'll need is praise, rewarding only when a series of exercises has been completed.

STAY ... JUST A LITTLE BIT LONGER

Train your puppy to stay with successive-approximation behavior shaping. From one second to 10 minutes, everything is done in small increments, allowing your dog to succeed at each level before moving on to the next. Always strive to let your puppy feel successful in everything he does. This will encourage him to continue performing, and

he'll look forward to working with you. Training should be fun for both of you.

When the fun stops, reassess your methods. Perhaps you need to change your approach; perhaps you just need to back up a little to regain a sense of achievement and fun. A common pitfall of the positive-reinforcement method is being so pleased by your puppy's success at one level that you move too quickly to the next level, before he clearly understands the current exercise or before you have firmly reinforced his success. Dogs are rarely disobedient because of choice. A lack of response is usually due to the dog misunderstanding what you want.

The stay exercises must be conducted in very small increments. Begin with short, second-by-second intervals, gradually increasing the time span with each exercise. Don't expect your puppy to remain in place for even 10 seconds on the first couple of rounds. Some dogs may surprise you and do so, but this is a shaky foundation for future success. Begin with a mere two seconds and gradually build on that. It might seem too easy, but that's the way it should be.

Easy equals success. Success equals joy in performance and the desire to continue.

There are three parts to a strong stay:

The first is time. Gradually increase the amount of time your dog is to remain in place.

The second is movement. Your puppy will learn to remain in one place as you move around him.

The third is distance. Your puppy will learn to remain in one place as you move around him and increase your distance from him.

THE SIT/STAY

Practice this exercise while facing your puppy, and from the heel position. Use the same visual cue and verbal cue regardless of where you are when giving the cue. Begin with your puppy in a sit position. Bridge and reward the second he sits. Bring your visual cue in front of his face as you give the stay cue. Your visual cue should be something clearly identifiable, like the palm of your hand with your fingers spread apart. Never swing your hand toward him, as your puppy will flinch and worry about it. Instead, bring your hand in from the side. There's no need to touch your dog with your hand. Always precede the cue with your dog's name.

If you are facing your puppy, remain in front. If you are performing the exercise from the heel position, step directly in front of your dog using the leg opposite of the one you use when going into the heel. For example, if you step forward on your left leg first for the heel excercise, step in front of your puppy on your right leg for the stay exercise.

Hold the target near your puppy's nose. As he remains in place, nose on target, praise him. After a mere two or three seconds, praise, click and reward, then continue into the heel again or release him from work. Do something other than try to make him continue sitting.

Within a few minutes, do the stay exercise again. This time have your puppy hold the position for five seconds prior to the bridge and reward. Always end the stay by moving on to something else. Don't just allow your dog to get up on his own.

If your puppy gets up at any time while you are doing the stay exercise, lure him back into position with the target (your hand) and repeat the stay cue, complete with a visual cue. While working on the initial stays of mere seconds, your puppy is less

All family members should be involved in training the new puppy. He needs to see that he has to obey everyone in the household, even the children.

Did You Know?

Roughly stated, targeting is the ability to recognize a visual target, then move to it, watch it or follow it. When a dog is chasing a flying disk, she uses targeting to track and anticipate the flight path. When a dog is heeling, she is targeting her handler's body to know where and when to move. Controlling a dog's movement with targets is not unique to clickertraining. However, clickertraining went beyond the simple use of food targets and unleashed our ability to teach precise behaviors beyond the reach of our arms and leashes.

You should always reward your puppy for a job well done, but treats aren't the only way to do so! Praise and playtime work too.

likely to break the position, but he may do so as you increase the time.

If your puppy repeatedly moves out of position, it means that you are trying to make him stay for longer than he is capable. In essence, it means you have breached his threshold for the exercise. Back up to where he worked successfully, and slowly increase the time from there.

Once your puppy can maintain the sit/stay for at least 45 seconds, begin adding movement. As with anything else, do this using successive approximation, meaning that you will gradually add more and more movement with each stay exercise.

Begin by moving from side to side while facing your puppy — just one step in each direction. Praise as he remains in position. Return to the heel position, praise, click and reward. Praising your dog while he stays will reinforce his behavior, which will maintain his attention on you and reassure him that he is doing what you want.

If this first foray into movement was successful, go to the next stage and move two steps in each direction. Again, praise throughout the excercise. Always click and reward upon returning to the heel position.

Once your puppy does well with you moving in front of him (still remaining close, mind you), begin moving along each side of him. Gradually increase your front-

It is extremely important that all family members are on the same page when it comes to training. Get everyone involved in the fun!

SMART TIP! Enroll in an obedience class if one is available in your area. Many localities have dog clubs that offer basic obedience training, as well as preparatory classes for obedience competitions.

to-back movement with each successful stay exercise. If he gets up and you have to reposition him at any time, go back a few steps and rebuild.

With success in moving along each side, you can then go on to moving completely around your dog. Alternate directions so your puppy doesn't become accustomed to only clockwise or counterclockwise movement. As you increase your movement throughout the stay exercise, continue to praise your dog, then return to the heel position or move him into another cue directly after you click and give him his reward.

MOVE BACK

Once you have taught your puppy to remain sitting for up to a minute while you walk all the way around him, you can introduce the third factor — distance. After all, what good is a stay if you can't walk away? If your puppy is solid in his sit/stay while you move around him, distance shouldn't pose a problem. However, if your dog is at all insecure or has separation issues, trying to gain distance can be tricky. You'll have to proceed a little slower, always aware of the particular point at which your puppy becomes unstable.

Begin by doing the sit/stay exercise at the level at which your dog is familiar. Remain close and walk around in both directions. You should be able to circle him at least three times before bridging and continuing to

another exercise. This will ensure that your puppy is ready for distance work.

Just as you moved around your puppy in ever-increasing increments, increase distance in the same way. On the first go-around, step away from your puppy just a foot or two while you walk around. Take care to step away but not straight back from him. Stepping back might cause your dog to get up and come toward you, since you have given body language similar to that of the come cue. To avoid this misunderstanding, gradually increase the distance as you walk around. Praise the entire time.

When you have done a complete circle at least once, bridge, reward and then go on to something else. The next time, increase the distance by a few more feet and try to circle him a couple of times. Within five or six sit/stay exercises, you should be able to be up to 6 feet away from your puppy as you walk around.

If your puppy keeps moving as you walk around him, try continuous targeting. This means keeping your hand near his nose as you move around him. You will need to bridge and reward more often, because your puppy can still feel insecure without this constant reinforcement. Very gradually, as your

NOTABLE & QUOTABLE

Remember that a dog functions in the here and now. The next second, her mind will be onto something else. You need to let your dog know exactly when the behavior is right and exactly when it's wrong. If your timing's off, you may inadvertently be training just what you don't want your dog to do!

— Fran Feldstein Culler, a trainer and obedience competitor from Auburn, Ind.

SMART TIP!

Keep in mind that dogs, like humans, have good days and bad days. Although frustrating, if you're aware that such ups and downs are simply part of training, your sessions will be more fun and more effective.

puppy learns that you will not be leaving him forever, you can take your target away briefly. Gradually increase the time that the target is not directly by his nose.

THE DOWN/STAY

Everything you did for the sit/stay applies to the down/stay, with slight modifications. Once your puppy is lying down,

present your visual stay cue and tell him to stay. Make him remain in position for only a few seconds, then click and reward. Move him out of the down position by either taking him forward into a heel or releasing him from work. If your puppy is at all difficult in the down position, it is best to offer a jackpot of rewards when he has remained in the down and then release him immediately, offering a generous belly rub. You'll need to make this behavior one of the most positive things your puppy can do. If he knows that lying down has a very positive outcome, he'll learn to ignore his instinct and respond to your cue.

In the beginning, just remain in the heel position with your hand near your puppy's shoulder blades. This will enable you to place him in the down position if he tries to get up. If he is constantly trying to get up, shorten the length of the down/stay and go back to the point where he remained as long as he was targeting. You may need to practice this for a few days prior to moving the target away.

Gradually shape your puppy's down/ stay until he can remain in place for a minute. This will ensure a solid behavior prior to adding more. If you move too soon, the punishment necessary to return your puppy to the down position might give your dog a negative feeling about the exercise. You're better off taking your time and getting it right.

When you reach the point where your puppy can remain in the down/stay for a minute, you can begin moving around him. The main difference between the sit/stay and the down/stay is that you should begin your movement at your dog's side during a down/stay instead of in front of him, as in the sit/stay.

Teaching the down/stay may prove to be challenging, but, continue rewarding every step of the way, and your puppy will understand in no time!

To be sure that your puppy will remain in the down/stay, you may want to roll his hips to the side. From this position, it takes him longer to get to his feet, and you'll have a visual cue that he's about to get up. With more time to lure him back into position, you can preempt his breaking the cue by returning him into position.

The first couple of movements should be along one side. Go a few steps toward his rear, then back into the heel position. Praise him the entire time he remains in position. This reinforces the behavior without ending the exercise. When you are ready to end the exercise, praise, click, reward and then continue on to something else.

The next time, try to get all the way behind your puppy. Praise him the entire time he remains in place, then return to his side, praise, click and reward, and move on to another behavior.

When your puppy can remain in the down/stay as you walk alongside and behind him, extend your path around the rear to his other side. Again, once he has learned to remain in place for this level of criteria, click, reward and continue to the next step — distance.

Within a few down/stay exercises you should be able to walk completely around your puppy and gradually increase your distance from him as you praise throughout his good responses. Your praise will encourage your puppy to remain in place, because he knows it's the right thing to do to receive the ultimate reward: a treat or a toy.

& STAND

Two additional basic cues – come and stand – are very useful for every puppy to learn.

Teaching your dog to come to you when called is arguably the most important of all cues. When he is reliably trained in this behavior, your puppy will gain loads of freedom and you will gain confidence in your beloved dog. The entire family can go to the park and allow your puppy to run and play. You can take him to the beach and let him swim. You can go on family camping or hiking trips and allow him to explore a bit. The possibilities are endless.

Standing still while being examined or bathed will be quite an accomplishment for your dog, and the stand cue will make your life much easier. You will appreciate his cooperation when you wipe his muddy feet, when you have him in the bathtub and while he's being examined by his veterinarian. Not only will this behavior make life with your puppy far easier for you, it will also make life easier for your puppy. A

Did You Know?

The rules that you use to govern your puppy's behavior are as much for your family as for your dog. Family-wide consistency is essential to achieving good results in training. Make sure everyone knows and follows the same rules with your puppy, or your best-laid plans will unravel.

dog who doesn't know what to expect or how to behave when something unexpected or stressful occurs can easily become frightened and uncooperative, whereas a dog who fully understands what is happening and what is expected of him will be totally relaxed.

THE COME CUE

Your puppy must learn to come to you regardless of what he is doing, where you are calling him from and what distractions are happening in his vicinity. This ultimate goal, like other trained responses, is best achieved by being broken down into small, manageable steps.

The first step is to perform a recall from a short distance, in an area where there are no distractions. Make certain that your puppy is on leash so that you can back up your cue if something distracts him (meaning that you can pull him toward you for a correct response if he fails to come on his own). It is unlikely that you'll have to apply any pressure on the leash if you use a lure and appropriate body language with a happy vocal tone. The lure can be food, a toy or crouching to his level while speaking in a welcoming voice.

Practice the short-distance recall from different stay positions and during your puppy's break time, when he's not working. Varying the conditions will reinforce his training-session responses.

During the exercise, do not put any pressure on the leash as you move around your dog. The slightest pressure can urge your puppy out of his stay before you want him to move. It will take some time and conditioning to teach your dog not to move when the leash is being tugged. He's not there yet, so be careful.

The next criterion is distance. To ensure success, start small by adding a mere 2 feet to the distance between you and your dog, who should be on leash (at this point 6 feet long), as he should be when you begin any new exercise.

Later, once your dog responds well to movement and distance, you can gradually increase the distractions while working (discussed in detail later), but for now try working with your puppy somewhere other than a quiet yard or room. Take a walk through the neighborhood, work in your front yard or go to a park. However, don't try to increase your distance by more than the 6 feet your leash allows. When you begin preparing for off-leash work, you'll increase your distances when working on stays and comes.

Start by showing your target to your puppy. Bridge and reward when he touches it with his nose. Pull the target closer to yourself as you bend at the waist or crouch to his level. Speak in a soothing, cheerful tone as you tell your

A well-trained puppy is a well-behaved one. Once you teach your puppy to respond on cue, it will make everything from bath time to playtime more enjoyable.

NOTABLE & QUOTABLE

In my experience, toy dogs are not the easiest to train, but you just have to figure out how to get through to them. With my first Japanese Chin, when the training got boring, he would just lie down. I learned to be a more enthusiastic trainer and train for shorter periods more frequently throughout the day. I would stop training when he was still eager, so he thought it was a really fun game. It worked. — dog owner Marisa Capozzo of North Middletown, N.J.

pup to come to you. Praise your puppy as he responds. When he arrives at your feet, praise, click and reward. Your puppy will learn this cue quickly if you make the reward worth it.

Repeat the exercise from 4 feet away. When that is successful, back up to 6 feet. Gradually increase the distance with each success. Make certain the recall is solid from all positions (his and yours) before you add more distance. Your puppy should come to you regardless of the direction you are calling him from. Always make your puppy's arrival as pleasant as possible, so that he always knows that coming to you is the best thing he could do.

Practicing the recall from a distance off leash will be tricky, as you have no means of backing up your cue or keeping your puppy from becoming more enthusiastic about another activity. Only pursue this if you are in a small, closed environ-ment where you can quickly regain your puppy's attention.

THE STAND CUE

Teaching your puppy to remain still while standing will be a bit of a challenge, but if you go about it in a gradual manner, taking small steps and building on them, you'll have a dog who will stand still and remain calm no matter where or when.

Placing your dog in the stand position will require both hands, so you won't be able to lure him into position, nor will you be able to use your clicker. If you have the time (and timing) to shape the behavior with only the clicker and treats, then you won't have to actually place your puppy into position, in which case you will be able to use these items.

The best teaching method begins by telling your puppy what you want — that

Food rewards during training sessions should be small and easy to eat, so that your puppy will stay focused on earning more.

Did You Know?

With clickertraining, the click sound marks the moment the desired behavior occurs and informs your dog that she earned a reward. Complex behaviors can be split into smaller parts for teaching, so your dog receives many rewards for each mini-step before adding more. Simple behaviors are then connected in sequence to produce the complex goal.

is, by placing him in the stand position. This minimizes misunderstanding and the likelihood that your puppy will exhibit different behaviors until he eventually does what you want.

There are several ways to teach the stand, depending on the starting point. From the sitting position, do the following:

1. Place the entire leash in the hand opposite the side on which your puppy is sitting. If he is on your left, put the leash in your right hand. If he is on your right, put the leash in your left hand.

2. As you say "stand," give a visual cue, such as gliding your hand from his nose, down his side to his loin area, then under his tummy to just below his rib cage, where your hand will remain.

3. As you gently pull forward on the leash, lift your puppy's rear end by putting pressure on the area, just below the rib cage. Be gentle; this is a sensitive area.

4. When your puppy is standing, place your hand holding the leash in front of his chest, and rub his tummy with the hand under his stomach as you praise him. Standing earns your puppy a tummy rub, which is just as pleasurable as a treat. You can also teach the stand cue when your puppy is already standing or walking with you. If your puppy is more than 50 pounds, you might want to begin with this method.

5. As you are walking or standing nearby, place the entire leash in the hand opposite the side where your puppy is walking or standing. Make sure you don't have the leash so tight that you pull on it. There should be at least 2, preferably 3, feet of leash between you and your puppy.

6. Using the same visual cue of moving your open-palmed hand from your puppy's nose, down his side, and then under his belly, say "stand." The main difference here is that your hand stops in front of his hind leg, around the thigh area, rather than under his belly. This will stop his forward movement. Once he has stopped, you can move your hand back to his tummy and rub it while your puppy receives his praise.

JOIN OUR
ONLINE
Club
Pup™

Clickertraining has elements of classical and operant conditioning.
Pairing the clicker with something the dog likes — a treat, toy or
praise — is an example of positive reinforcement. Log on to
DogChannel.com/Club-Pup to find out more about clickertraining.
Just click on "Downloads."

1. Have your puppy heel with you. As you stop, praise, click and reward before he has a chance to sit. Be sure to pair this action with the stand cue.

2. Repeat this exercise up to five times. You'll need to temporarily phase out the automatic sit, if your puppy is so inclined at this time.

3. Gradually increase the time between your stand cue and the click and praise. This will increase your puppy's behavior threshold, meaning that he will learn to maintain standing a little longer each time it is requested.

4. Add the word "stay" to the behavior chain. For example, tell him to stand as you stop. While he is waiting for his bridging signal (click), tell him to stay.

Your puppy already has a good idea of what is expected when you tell him to stay. He'll most likely know that he's not supposed to move. Gradually add the praise, as he remains in place for longer and longer. Wait until the behavior is complete, then click and give the food or toy reward.

If it helps to maintain the stand position by rubbing your dog's tummy, go ahead and do so, gradually decreasing the contact as your puppy becomes comfortable with the stand/stay exercise.

it's a Fact

Dogs are wired to keep doing behaviors that produce positive results and to avoid the behaviors that don't. This is why they're such a successful species. Imagine, they went from wolves to wild dogs to creatures that share our homes. That's remarkable. And we're the ones providing them with food, water, shelter and love. What a good deal for the dog! But, obeying her owner isn't an intuitive thing for a dog, especially when it comes to basic obedience. You have to show your dog that doing what you ask brings wonderful rewards and that, above all, it is fun, fun, fun.

Clickertraining has elements of classical and operant conditioning.
Pairing the clicker with something the dog likes — a treat, toy or
praise — is an example of positive reinforcement. Log on to
DogChannel.com/Club-Pup to find out more about clickertraining.
Just click on "Downloads."

JOIN OUR
ONLINE
**Club
Pup**™

1. Have your puppy heel with you. As you stop, praise, click and reward before he has a chance to sit. Be sure to pair this action with the stand cue.

2. Repeat this exercise up to five times. You'll need to temporarily phase out the automatic sit, if your puppy is so inclined at this time.

3. Gradually increase the time between your stand cue and the click and praise. This will increase your puppy's behavior threshold, meaning that he will learn to maintain standing a little longer each time it is requested.

4. Add the word "stay" to the behavior chain. For example, tell him to stand as you stop. While he is waiting for his bridging signal (click), tell him to stay.

Your puppy already has a good idea of what is expected when you tell him to stay. He'll most likely know that he's not supposed to move. Gradually add the praise, as he remains in place for longer and longer. Wait until the behavior is complete, then click and give the food or toy reward.

If it helps to maintain the stand position by rubbing your dog's tummy, go ahead and do so, gradually decreasing the contact as your puppy becomes comfortable with the stand/stay exercise.

it's a Fact

Dogs are wired to keep doing behaviors that produce positive results and to avoid the behaviors that don't. This is why they're such a successful species. Imagine, they went from wolves to wild dogs to creatures that share our homes. That's remarkable. And we're the ones providing them with food, water, shelter and love. What a good deal for the dog! But, obeying her owner isn't an intuitive thing for a dog, especially when it comes to basic obedience. You have to show your dog that doing what you ask brings wonderful rewards and that, above all, it is fun, fun, fun.

JOIN OUR ONLINE Club Pup™

Clickertraining has elements of classical and operant conditioning. Pairing the clicker with something the dog likes — a treat, toy or praise — is an example of positive reinforcement. Log on to **DogChannel.com/Club-Pup** to find out more about clickertraining. Just click on "Downloads."

SMART TIP!

Treats should be small, soft bits — some companies now make training treats just for this purpose. You can also use small bits of cheese, beef, chicken or anything else easy to swallow in one gulp. The idea is to have your dog eat the goodie just after she has done what you wanted; if your dog is crunching away on a hard treat, she's not processing how she got the treat. She should eat the small treat, then immediately try to find a way to get another one by repeating the behavior you want.

STAND/STAY COMBO

Before you can expect your puppy to remain in a stand while being examined or bathed, he'll need to learn to remain in the position as you move around him or walk away. Teaching the stand/stay is helpful to all dogs but especially considerate to old dogs. Many older dogs' hind legs and hips tend to be arthritic, making sitting difficult. Requesting a stand/stay allows an older dog to perform without stressing his joints. A step-by-step progression for teaching the stand/stay appears below.

1. To begin, have your puppy stand before you.

2. Place the leash either on the ground in front of him (if you're certain he's not in the mood to go anywhere) or place it between your knees.

3. Keeping your hand under his tummy and rubbing his belly slowly, place your other hand in front of his face and give him the same visual cue you used in training the previous stays, saying your puppy's name, then "stay."

4. Make him hold this position for 10 to 15 seconds, then go directly into a heel. Gradually increase this stay time with each successful stay exercise.

5. When your puppy is reliably standing still with you rubbing his tummy for up to a minute, it's time to add movement.

6. Begin by moving toward his rear, still touching his tummy or keeping your hand in front of one of his hind legs. Make this movement brief, then return to the heel position, praise him, and go forward into the heel position.

7. Repeat this three or four times until your puppy maintains the stand/stay very reliably. Then add some more movement. Go behind him and around to his other side, always rubbing his tummy.

8. Repeat this three or four times, then make a complete circle around him (still rubbing his tummy, which keeps him stable and in one spot; your puppy is unlikely to move during a tummy rub).

9. As you move around him, briefly remove your hand from under his tummy. If he looks around at you, put your hand back briefly, then remove it again. Once you can make a complete circle around your puppy without touching him, you're ready for step 10.

10. Gradually add distance as you move around your puppy. Be certain to move in both directions so that he acclimates to your movements anywhere around him.

SHAPING A STAND/STAY

If you have already managed to shape another behavior with a bridge (such as a clicker response), then teaching your puppy how to stand and stay using the same techniques shouldn't be difficult. It's simply a matter of breaking the exercise down into smaller components.

6 Steps to Training Success

Training mistakes are common but easy to avoid if you know what you're doing. Here is some expert advice to help you avoid mistakes, so you and your puppy can win the training game.

1. Don't Punish.

Physical punishment is never appropriate for any breed of dog. It is unwise and ineffective to use yelling as punishment. This can really damage your relationship with your puppy. Clearly, the same applies to physical punishment. Wouldn't you rather have your dog comply because she wants to, instead of because she's afraid of you?

2. Be Realistic.

Novice trainers need to realize that dogs don't understand our language. Most training problems are a result of the handler asking the dog to do something she doesn't understand. Once the dog truly understands a cue, then a handler can expect the dog to perform and can judiciously apply some negative reinforcement if the performance is inadequate. The negative reinforcement can be merely withholding food and your praise.

3. Give the Reward.

If you don't reward your puppy's efforts, you are going to get shoddy results. Just like if your boss didn't pay you for your work, you might not get your work done as quickly.

4. Be Consistent.

Be consistent and don't confuse your puppy with mixed messages. Your puppy can't understand why she can jump on your friends on Saturdays when they're wearing blue jeans and not on New Year's Eve when they're dressed their finest. Ignoring a behavior one day and scolding for it another is not fair to your puppy.

5. Be Clear the First Time.

The worst thing an owner can do is to repeat the cue if the dog isn't complying. Often, dogs don't comply because they don't understand the cue in the current context, and repeating it just turns it into a word the dog hears while she's standing around; "Sit, sit, sit, sit" turns into background noise. If your dog is just learning a new behavior and isn't doing it, perhaps the environment is different from the one in which she learned, such as being in the park instead of the kitchen.

6. Don't Assume.

If your dog is having a difficult time learning a cue, go back to the basics. Just because your dog did it before doesn't mean she has the cue down pat. Think of obedience as a sport in which the athlete needs to practice. Little Leaguers don't hit homers once and then automatically know how to do it regularly.

1. Have your puppy heel with you. As you stop, praise, click and reward before he has a chance to sit. Be sure to pair this action with the stand cue.

2. Repeat this exercise up to five times. You'll need to temporarily phase out the automatic sit, if your puppy is so inclined at this time.

3. Gradually increase the time between your stand cue and the click and praise. This will increase your puppy's behavior threshold, meaning that he will learn to maintain standing a little longer each time it is requested.

4. Add the word "stay" to the behavior chain. For example, tell him to stand as you stop. While he is waiting for his bridging signal (click), tell him to stay.

Your puppy already has a good idea of what is expected when you tell him to stay. He'll most likely know that he's not supposed to move. Gradually add the praise, as he remains in place for longer and longer. Wait until the behavior is complete, then click and give the food or toy reward.

If it helps to maintain the stand position by rubbing your dog's tummy, go ahead and do so, gradually decreasing the contact as your puppy becomes comfortable with the stand/stay exercise.

it's a **Fact**

Dogs are wired to keep doing behaviors that produce positive results and to avoid the behaviors that don't. This is why they're such a successful species. Imagine, they went from wolves to wild dogs to creatures that share our homes. That's remarkable. And we're the ones providing them with food, water, shelter and love. What a good deal for the dog! But, obeying her owner isn't an intuitive thing for a dog, especially when it comes to basic obedience. You have to show your dog that doing what you ask brings wonderful rewards and that, above all, it is fun, fun, fun.

Properly trained come, sit and stay cues could save your pup's life.

TRAINING

Everything that you and your pup have learned to this point has prepared you for working with your puppy in the real world without having to rely on a training device or leash, communicating solely with visual cues and your voice. You began training in a closed space or on leash so that you would have the means to follow through with all of the cues. This convinced your puppy that you were always "on top of your game" and gave you the confidence that he will reliably do his part.

To successfully transfer from working on a leash to working without one, you will need good timing for your verbal and visual cues, as well as a puppy who is completely resistant to distractions. The training designed to reach that goal is gradual, like your puppy's training thus far, so that he will have no idea that he's off leash but will still respond to you.

it's a Fact

As your puppy advances in her training and as she ages, she will behave more reliably off leash for longer periods of time. Eventually, your dog will only need to be on leash when you take her to places where leashes are mandatory, such as parks, city centers or other areas where laws mandate that dogs be on leash at all times.

There are three prerequisites to letting go of the leash:

1. Know Thyself. To teach your dog to correct himself, use the finish exercise. The finish will put your dog back into the heel position whenever he isn't there but should be.

2. Speak and Be Heard: This prerequisite allows you to be able to use a mere verbal correction when your puppy begins to move out of position or doesn't respond as he should. This is called "leash reduction." Your puppy must learn that your voice has just as much power as a treat or a leash pull. In essence, you'll be able to guide your puppy by saying either "good" or "no," just as you responded to verbal cues in that "hot and cold" or "stop and go" game you played as a child.

3. Conquer Space: This entails getting him to listen to you when you are standing a long distance away from him. He'll need to be able to come when called, sit, lie down and stay when you move more than 20 feet away. Your puppy must learn that you have ultimate control, regardless of where you are and whether he sees you or not. This means that you and your puppy will need to do long-leash work before you graduate to off-leash work.

Once your puppy starts obeying you while you are out of sight a longer distance away and without the use of the

Advancing your training techniques will help strengthen your puppy's understanding of obedience cues.

leash, he will be ready to continue work without a leash.

THE FINISH CUE

Although this might be a new exercise to you, it really isn't new to your puppy. It is simply the heeling exercise in reverse.

Did You Know?

A front-connecting body harness can be used instead of a collar. It fastens with adjustable straps across a dog's chest and behind her front legs. Several styles are available, but most have a metal D-ring to clip the leash to the strap at the dog's chest. If your dog pulls while wearing the harness, her chest takes the weight instead of her throat, so no pressure is applied to your dog's airway. This is especially helpful for flat-faced dogs and those with fragile necks.

The finish is used when you want your pup to be in a heel but he isn't. Let's say you are heeling with him and you stop. Instead of sitting at your side, he steps in front of you and sits. Or you have called him to come, and he comes and sits in front of you, as he should, but you wish to move forward. In either case, you should have him perform a finish so that you are both facing the same direction.

In essence, the finish will keep your puppy's attention on you, instead of letting him go his own way. The more you do to keep his attention, the better. With attentiveness, you don't need training devices.

There are two ways to do a finish. The method you use depends on your dog.

You can finish to the left or to the right. A left finish is easier with a small dog or one who can maneuver in small circles (such as a Sheltie, an Australian Shepherd or a Border Collie) and the right finish with a larger dog or one that tends to stop way in front of you.

To finish to the left:

1. Place half of the leash in your left hand, along with some bait (aka treats). The other half of the leash should be between your hand and your puppy's collar. Show your puppy the bait.

2. As you step back on your left leg, swing your left arm out and then back while you are giving your puppy the heel cue.

SMART TIP!

Regardless of the work it takes to get your puppy to come to you, never show displeasure of any sort when she arrives. Always be happy and praise her, even if she came on her own from a mere 2 feet away.

3. Your puppy will move after the bait and your leg movement.

4. Once his body is even with your left leg, bring your left arm forward to be even with your left side and bring your left leg up to be even with your right.

5. As your dog moves up your left side, tell him to sit just before he arrives in the heel position.

To finish to the right:

1. Place half of the leash in your right hand. Make sure the other half is between you and your puppy's collar.

2. As you step backward on your right leg, tell him to heel or use whatever word you choose for this exercise. Don't move your left leg. Keep it cemented in place (pretend to, anyway).

3. Your movement back will entice your puppy to also move in that direction along your right side. If he doesn't, then take two more steps back. (You'll need to *un-*cement your left foot and replace it when you return to your former position.)

4. When your puppy begins to move along your right leg, bring it back into position even with your left leg, as you pass the leash behind your back to your left hand.

5. As your puppy reaches your left heel, tell him to sit. Don't wait. The cue takes a few seconds to travel from the dog's ear canal through the brain, to the muscles, and finally to the action. If your puppy is extremely slow on the uptake, tell him to sit even sooner.

If your puppy ends up in front of you again, do the finish again. If this happens repeatedly, make sure to either bait him or place him into position. Baiting is the easiest solution, but you'll have to place your dog in position if he isn't motivated by food or toys.

You may need to repeat this a few times before you both have the finish cue mastered. Good timing is essential. If you use a clicker to bridge your signals, keep it in your right hand and click when he sits at your side. Using a clicker might be difficult if finishing to the right, unless you're dexterous.

LEASH REDUCTION

There really isn't any magic to leash reduction; it just takes repetition and persistence. Through repetition, your dog will learn how to perform according to your standards. Through persistence, you will always get the response you want out of your puppy.

Turns are the name of the game. Turn left when your puppy is behind you or on the wrong side of you, and turn right when he is in front of you. Just before you turn, say the word "no" in a low tone of voice. Soon, your puppy will identify that word with the need to watch you more closely and correct himself. The "no" alone will make him return to proper heeling position without any leash correction or turn.

Your turns should be fast and should not follow any pattern. The more erratic you make your walking speeds and turn directions, the more attentive your dog will be. Dogs actually love being challenged in this way. To your puppy, it becomes a fun game.

Within a few weeks, your puppy should be heeling at your side with little use for any leash correction. Now he's ready to begin his long-leash work.

LONG DISTANCE

Before you begin your long-leash work, you'll need a 15- to 20-foot leash. Practice gathering it before you even put it on your puppy. Gather from the clip-end out to give you the most leash control.

Grab the leash in both hands. Slide it through one hand and bring it together in the other, releasing and sliding through again until it is fully gathered. Once the leash is gathered, put the hand nearest your dog on the leash, 3 feet from his collar. Put the remainder of the leash in the other hand so that you aren't slapping your dog in the face with a dangling leash.

The purpose of long-distance training is to teach your puppy to stay and come from far away and out of sight. Wouldn't it be nice for your puppy to remain with you in your yard while you talk to a neighbor or work in the garden?

Stays: Once your puppy is on the long

leash and you are comfortably holding it gathered, practice your down/stays and sit/stays, gradually increasing the distance by spiraling around your dog. Don't go straight out or your puppy might think you're about to call him. Spiraling out will make your increasing distance less noticeable to him. Be sure to go around your dog in both directions, so that he accepts movement all around him.

If your puppy moves out of his stay position at any time, immediately say "no" in a low tone of voice as you go directly to him and return him to his proper position. Don't worry about what your long leash is doing. Either use bait to lure him back into position or take the leash near his collar and gently place him into his original position. Don't grab your dog's collar, as he will perceive it as a very threatening movement. Gradually work your way outward again.

Don't try to reach 15 or 20 feet on the first try. You may not even make it on the second try. Take your time and gradually build distance to ensure that your puppy's stays are very solid. If there's a point at which he keeps getting up, back up a bit to a distance where he's comfortable and reliable. Work at this level for a while, and gradually increase the distance again in small increments.

Recall (Come When Called): Before starting this exercise from a distance, be sure that your puppy is reliable from the end of your 6-foot leash. He should be able to come directly to you from any direction and sit in front of you. He should also reliably perform this exercise when distracted. Distraction-proofing

the recall is extremely important; if he isn't reliable from 6 feet away, he surely won't be reliable from 20 feet away.

At the same time that you gradually increase the distance in your stay exercises, do the same in your recall exercises. Do a recall after every one or two stays. Practice with your puppy from different directions and varying distances.

As your puppy comes toward you, gather your leash quickly. If he comes faster than you can gather, have his reward ready; make sure he sits when he arrives, then give it to him. As he's eating the treat or playing with the toy, take your leash, leaving 3 feet of slack between you and your puppy's collar, and do your finish. Once done, the leash will no longer be between your puppy's legs, which will allow you to gather it as you move forward into a heel.

When your dog reliably stays and performs the recall from 20 feet away, it's time to drop the leash. The key is for your puppy to still believe that you have the leash when you really don't. Since he has been conditioned to listen from a distance, he should continue to do so when you move farther away. Since your leash is only 20 feet long, though, you will have to drop it.

There is an art to dropping the leash. Dogs are atuned to our body language. They can tell when you let go of the leash. Some won't care because they are having too much fun training, but others may try to take advantage of the situation. So, make sure you drop the leash nonchalantly. Let go as you are moving around your puppy; don't announce your intent by stopping to lay the leash down. When your upper body bends over, your dog can misconstrue your body language

as a recall request. He might break his stay and come toward you, instead of remaining in place as you desired.

The first time you walk around your dog, remain at the constant distance you reached when you were holding the leash (at a radius of 20 feet). Keep a sharp eye on your puppy, and praise him occasionally as you walk. If he moves his weight onto his shoulders, he's in the process of getting up. When you see this, go directly to him and either lure him back with a reward or take hold of his leash near the collar and replace him in position, reiterating the stay cue. If he relaxes back onto his haunches before you return, be sure to praise him. You don't have to give the cue again; he's well aware of it.

Once your puppy resettles into position, gradually move away from him again. You should still back away in a spiral motion because walking straight back will make

Did You Know?

Several types of leashes can be used for training loose-leash walking. Most are available in leather, nylon and cotton.

■ **6-foot leash:** This can be used either shortened or full-length, and it is long enough to tie to your belt for hands-free walking.

■ **4-foot leash:** This is similar to the 6-foot leash but less versatile.

■ **10- to 30-foot long line:** The long line allows safe control, while giving your dog freedom to explore.

■ **Retractable lead:** This is handy, but it's operated by the dog pulling. Retractable leads directly reinforce (reward) pulling on the leash. This counteracts what you're trying to teach.

him more aware that you're moving away. At this level of distance work, you don't want your actions to be obvious. Your dog will accept increasing behavioral thresholds and listen better if you are subtle.

As your puppy reliably responds to your training with the leash dropped at 20 feet, gradually increase your distance with each successive stay exercise. You can do this during down/stays or sit/stays. Vary them often and practice your recall exercises from different locations around him. The more you vary the exercises, the more reliable your dog will

be. Dogs bore easily. Variation maintains their attention longer.

At this point, your recall procedures should also change a bit. Instead of trying to gather your leash, leave the leash on the ground. Step on the end and then call your dog to you. You are stepping on the end of the leash as a precaution. Your puppy may not be 100-percent reliable on the recall in every situation. Having weight on the leash will deter him if he decides to go in any direction other than straight to you or if he does not respond at all. You still need a means of enforcing your cue, and holding the leash beneath your feet will help.

If all goes well when you call your puppy, he should arrive facing you at your feet. Praise and reward him, then grasp the leash near his collar and perform the finish, allowing you to disentangle him and gather the leash as you move forward into the heel.

If your puppy decides not to come when called, do the following: As you move backward (your backward movement is a beckoning gesture, which entices your puppy to come to you), give the leash a little tug and coax him to you using a pleasant tone of voice. Don't repeat the cue or else it will teach him that your first command meant nothing. Merely show him that things are far more pleasant when he comes to you than when he chooses to go elsewhere or simply not to listen.

As you move backward, the leash will automatically tug against him. However, if there's an enticing distraction nearby, such as another dog, a child or a toy, your puppy might find the distraction to be more attractive than moving toward you. Tug gently on the leash, use your low-toned "no" correction and continue moving backward until he comes toward you. Stop, wait for his arrival, and praise him the entire time that he's

JOIN OUR ONLINE Club Pup™

Shaping involves allowing a dog to offer a behavior on her own, while you offer praise for slight movements toward a desired behavior. Learn more about how to shape a neat trick called "sorry" by downloading the steps at **DogChannel.com/Club-Pup;** just click on "Downloads" and then "Shaping a Sorry."

coming toward you. This will communicate to your puppy that he is doing the right thing. Bridge and reward the moment he arrives and sits facing you.

When your puppy reliably comes to you from 20 feet away when prompted, regardless of distractions, begin doing the recall without stepping on the leash. If you are in an unfenced area, try tieing the end of the leash to a tree or putting it under a rock or another solid object. No response is 100-percent guaranteed, and this is a safety measure in case your puppy is defiant. When you call your puppy to you, also make sure he won't pull on his leash when responding. Once he's completed the recall, heel with him to where you tied the end of the leash; untie it and gather as you walk with him.

As you progress to training your puppy to stay and come without having to be near the leash, you can go back to your 6-foot-long leash, decreasing the amount of leash you must handle while training. If you train in an open area, however, it's best to use the long leash — just in case you need it.

Another tool you can begin using is the pull tab. It's essentially a very short leash, approximately 3-inches (for small/miniature dogs) to 6-inches long. It can make your puppy feel like he is still on his leash, while also giving you something to grab, if necessary. You can leave the pull tab on throughout the training session and even use it as the only leash still on when you do your stay and recall exercises. It will also come into play while teaching your puppy to heel off leash.

OFF-LEASH HEELING

This might be the most difficult behavior to accomplish without a leash, especially if you have continued to apply pressure through constant pulling or guiding with the

Once your puppy is well trained, you will have the confidence to let him explore the world around him because, no matter what, he will listen to you.

NOTABLE & QUOTABLE

Don't put a question mark at the end of a cue. Use your voice. One cue per dog. Do not repeat the cue — ever. The dog heard you; you are dominant. If you act afraid, you've lost the battle. — Sharon L. Perry, owner and director of training for Southern Star Ranch K9 Training Center in Florence, Texas

leash instead of using your vocal and visual cues. The key to achieving the off-lead heel is to use the leash sparingly while teaching your puppy his basics.

You'll know your puppy is ready for this exercise if you rarely have to use the leash to correct his heeling position. If he moves in front of you a bit, you should only need to use a verbal correction or a turn to make him fall back into place. Your puppy should perform in this manner regardless of where he is and what is going on around him. He should be attentive at all times.

While you have your puppy's attention, try dropping the leash as he heels. The leash will trail behind him, conveniently allowing you to step on it should your puppy decide to forge ahead. The weight

of the leash will also act as a slowing mechanism to deter your puppy from moving out of position. If the weight of the leash proves too distracting, switch to the pull tab. The tab will dangle from his collar, but you will have to be quick if you need to use it.

Be consistent with your puppy's heeling position. If you're too relaxed and get sloppy, it will lead to a deterioration of the exercise. The second your dog is out of position, use your verbal correction, followed immediately by a turn in the opposite direction, and apply pressure on the pull tab if the turn isn't sufficient to regain your dog's attention. If you wait until he is out of reach to chase after him, it could undo a lot of hard work.

Keep training sessions short, positive and upbeat. It's key to keeping your puppy's attention throughout.

NOTABLE &
QUOTABLE

Dogs need to know what they can and can't do. The dog should look to the owner for permission to do anything. The owner is the gatekeeper. The dog should never be allowed to do whatever he wants, whenever he wants. If there are no rules and structure for the dog, the dog is going to assume that [leadership] role.

— Caroline Haldeman, dog owner/trainer in Yorba Linda, Calif.

Forcing your puppy to do what you want him to do isn't the right solution. You need patience and a positive approach.

It's tough to find a puppy who doesn't have at least one behavioral problem. Count on misbehavior at one point or another. If you obtained your dog through a shelter or rescue group, it's a pretty safe bet that he'll have some behavioral issues. Even older dogs who have been relatively problem-free can develop undesirable behaviors later in life.

Regardless of your dog's age or the cause of his behavioral aberration, you need to address the issue and correct it. Be consistent and always show your puppy how pleased you are with correct behavior patterns.

JUMPING UP

Jumping up would not be an issue if you had never reinforced the behavior in any manner. It might be cute when your puppy is a small, but when he grows bigger and has muddy paws, it's no longer cute. If your response to a behavior is inconsistent, your puppy won't know it is not allowed. If he's received some sort of attention for doing it, the behavior has been rewarded.

In short, sooner is better when extinguishing an unwanted behavior. Here is the first key to extinction: Don't give your puppy any attention — positive or negative — when he jumps up. This means no touching, no speaking. These are positive responses. Don't push your dog off of you or yell, either. These are negative responses. Even the negative responses reward an attention-starved dog.

To avoid rewarding your puppy for jumping, turn away or step back. Continue to do so as long as he jumps. If this doesn't work, you'll need to apply some sort of negative reinforcement, such as a noise box or a spray of water in the face. You can easily make a noise box out of a small metal can with a handful of pennies inside. When your puppy jumps up, shake the can in an up-and-down motion once or twice. The noise will startle him, and he'll stop jumping. If your dog is ultrasensitive to noises, don't use this method. Instead, try filling a spray bottle or squirt gun with water and spritzing him in the face as he jumps.

Redirection is another key to behavior extinction. You need to divert your puppy's attention to something positive, such as sitting for attention. To be effective, redirection must be immediate and fully rewarded the second it is accomplished.

Most of us would prefer our dogs to sit when they want attention instead of incessantly jumping on us. Once you have stopped the jumping by turning away or using a means of negative reinforcement, tell your puppy to sit. The second his bottom touches the floor, praise, click and pet him. Each time he comes to sit near you, reward him with petting and praise. You don't have to have a clicker or squeaker to reinforce this behavior. In this case, touch is enough reward to promote the appropriate behavior routine. Just be certain that you're aware of your puppy's new attention-seeking pattern and that you reward him for it, or he'll go back to jumping up on you because he knows jumping up is sure to elicit some type of reaction.

TREASURE HUNTING

Doggie dumpster-diving is a tough behavior to extinguish. The garbage is a canine treasure trove. The food reward alone is enough to promote the behavior. You can't possibly mask the smells coming from the con-

tainer, and there is no way to keep your pup out entirely unless you put it somewhere inaccessible (and inconvenient for you). This can be arranged but hiding the trash will not overcome the dog's desire for treasure seeking. A dog can't easily ignore a tantalizing scent.

You will have to make the consequence of his inappropriate action dire enough or make an alternative even more attractive, if you want your dog to discontinue the behavior. It's tough to come up with some-

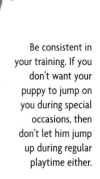

Be consistent in your training. If you don't want your puppy to jump on you during special occasions, then don't let him jump up during regular playtime either.

Dealing with a behavior that is based in strong emotion, such as aggression and fear, and with hardwired behavior, such as chasing things that move, can be daunting. Change these responses through counter conditioning — programming a new response to stimulus by giving it a new association. Download an alternate training method at **DogChannel.com/Club-Pup**.

thing more attractive than steak bones and leftover peas, so the best tactic is to teach your puppy not to go near the garbage can. Make it as off limits as your leather sofa, designer shoes or other prized possessions. Regardless of the temptation, your puppy can be taught to keep his mouth and paws off.

To condition your dog to leave your valuables (including your trash cans) alone, you'll need to apply some type of adverse effect when he nears or shows interest in these objects, such as a squirt of water or a startling sound. Then, guide him into a more positive action by using one of his own toys to get his attention and rewarding him with praise when he redirects his focus. Again, a combination of tactics applied repetitively and persistently will be the most effective; your puppy will get a bad vibe from the no-no object and good vibes when he avoids the object and goes for a toy.

You will have to be watchful and diligent to catch your dog in the act of sniffing the garbage. This includes subtle preliminary behavior such as sniffing the air nearby or putting his nose to the ground and gradually tracking his way in that direction. Catch him in the act of thinking about that enticing smell, and curb the inclination before it becomes an action, thereby making the limits clear to him. Communication is the key to reliability, as are consistency and praise.

EXCESSIVE BARKING

Barking is another self-rewarding behavior. It will take something far more attractive or very aversive to stop a dog from excessive barking. Yelling at him to be quiet just adds to the fun; to your dog, it just means you've joined in the bark fest.

You can redirect some dogs from the annoying behavior with various positive reinforcement shaping techniques, but others

get so much joy out of barking that they won't care what treats, toys or activities you use as bait. There are other dogs who will be quiet while you are around but sound off when you're not home. These dogs are more likely territorial barkers. They feel an instinctive duty to keep strangers at bay, even if the strangers are squirrels or sparrows. To such a dog, an intruder is a trespasser, no matter the size or species.

Some dogs bark because of separation anxiety. You can be pretty sure your dog has this disorder if he's quiet and relaxed when you're home, but exasperated neighbors report that your dog has spent the day barking at nothing. This type of barking is probably the most difficult to cure. The more the dog is punished for the behavior, the worse it becomes. This doesn't mean it can't be cured. Using homeopathic treatments and behavior-modification tactics usually works.

To cure excessive barking using positive reinforcement, you'll need to be consistent and dedicated. If you're using food as a reward, it's probably best to use your

Teach your dog to stay a distance away from the table while you eat. Give her a mat or position it at a [nearby] doorway where the flooring is different [from the flooring in the kitchen]. Then, each time your pup puts a paw on the kitchen floor, remind her to back up until all four paws are on the right surface. At first, you will need to be vigilant about supervising, but soon your dog will learn to wait until the meal is over before approaching.

— Colleen Pelar, a certified dog trainer from Springfield, Va.

SMART TIP!

Use this teething recipe to ease your puppy's teething pain and to occupy him for a while:

Pour chicken broth into an ice-cube tray. If you would like, add bits of meat, biscuit or other treats. Freeze, then give the frozen treats to your puppy.

puppy's regular kibble; otherwise, you'll fill him up with treats and he won't want to eat his normal meals.

Before you begin, arm yourself with a pouch or bag to carry a supply of kibble, a squeak toy and a clicker. The squeaker will act as a distraction, the clicker will reinforce the appropriate behavior and the kibble will reward the appropriate behavior.

Put your puppy in a situation in which he would normally bark. Praise, click and reward while he's quiet. If he barks, use the squeaker until he stops to investigate. When he does so, praise, click and reward again. Repeat throughout the training session.

Each time you put your puppy in a barking situation, have your tools close at hand. Use them consistently, and be patient. It will take some time for him to overcome a self-rewarding behavior such as barking.

STEALING

Stealing behavior is loosely linked to the chewing routine. Once your puppy steals a sock or shoe, he's found himself a delectable new chew treat. Often, stealing is a means of obtaining attention. Your puppy has learned that if he runs away with something he's not supposed to have, he'll launch a great game of tag.

There are several ways to handle this problem. Try to reward your puppy for playing with his own toys by joining in on the game. You will also have to ignore your pup when he steals your laundry and takes off with it; retrieve the items at a later time, and don't chase after him in the moment. A dog usually steals an item to start the racing mayhem that follows the mischief, rather than to chew on it. However, if your puppy likes to destroy the spoils of his larceny, you will have to reclaim the object pretty quickly. Redirection won't work because the stolen property is reward enough to cause the behavior.

Instead, keep your puppy on a leash. Don't allow him to go anywhere that you cannot observe him. When he sniffs at or lunges for something he isn't supposed to have, grab the leash and tell him to come. Reward him with praise, and try to interest him in a game with one of his own toys. Better yet, give him an interactive toy to occupy his time, such as a cube or ball that releases treats while the dog plays with it, a hollow shank bone that is filled with goodies or a rubber toy that is stuffed with something yummy. In this manner, you can redirect your puppy in a positive way, showing him that playing with his own toys is far more rewarding than going after something else.

Barking is a self-rewarding behavior, so you'll need to arm yourself with a clicker, edible treats and squeaky toys to help distract and redirect your puppy's excessive barking.

COUNTER SURFING

Counter surfing is another self-rewarding behavior, as it always yields a reward of some sort. It's going to be tough to convince your puppy not to do this.

The best way to avoid this negative behavior is to keep your counters clear of things that your puppy can eat and/or play with. In essence, clear the counters! With nothing to cause temptation, there will be no reason for him to counter surf other than to grab your attention.

You can only correct counter-surfing behavior when you are there to witness it. Therefore, don't give your puppy access to the kitchen or bathrooms when you can't watch him. Keep him on his leash at all times, so that you can quickly redirect his behavior. He shouldn't be allowed to put his paws on the countertop or table while you try to redirect or tempt him with a treat, as this can serve to further encourage him.

Often, a noise box will be enough to discourage your dog. Shake the can, and give a low-toned verbal reprimand. With consistency and persistence, this should work.

A scat mat can also do the trick. This is a device that emits brief electrical pulses, similar to static electricity, when the animal touches it. It is a strong enough deterrent to stop counter surfers. Scat mats are often used for cats, placed in doorways of rooms where the owners do not want their cats to enter. The mat is a negative reinforcement tool and something that your dog will want to avoid.

Is your puppy a laundry bandit? The best response to your little canine thief is no response at all. If you don't wait to retrieve your belongings until after he's moved on to another distraction, you will have taught him a new game to get your attention.

Did You Know?

Puppies explore with their mouths. Humans are oriented toward exploring and manipulating with their hands. Puppies' exploratory talents include carrying, licking, grabbing, biting and gnawing. Since these are skills an adult dog will need, they are also the skills a young dog needs to perfect. Unfortunately, young dogs try to perfect their skills on your new shoes, antique furniture and feather pillows.

You can also use a similar technique to the one for discouraging your pup from rushing to the door: Redirect him with a squeaker. When your puppy looks at you, you should praise, click and reward.

With nothing to reward him on the counter, he'll soon learn that all rewards come from you — the treat trader — which will make him pay attention to you instead of searching the counters for gratification.

CAT CHASING

When dogs and cats come face-to-face, few cats stand their ground — most run. And if it moves, your puppy will chase it. Dogs are hunters. Movement catches their eye, triggering the prey drive, which is an instinctive reaction to movement.

Obedience training is the first step toward controlling chasing behavior. Until your puppy is fully trained to listen to you and control himself, keep him on a leash when he is near the cat. When he shows interest in the cat, redirect him to his toys and to interacting with you. Through conditioning, you can teach him to respond appropriately.

Often, that's not the end of the matter, though. Many cats take advantage when they see a dog isn't able to go after them or has been conditioned not to react. Cats aren't stupid; some will tease. It's tough for a dog to ignore a flicking tail under his nose. Provided your cat has a means of safely escaping from your puppy, allow your puppy to follow the cat. Observe as each animal establishes his boundaries. Who knows? They might become playmates!

RUSHING THE DOOR

A dog may rush the door for territorial reasons or to give an happy greeting. The method you use to cure the problem depends on the reason for the behavior. Be sure to observe your puppy's overall behavior patterns to determine why he's rushing the door.

A territorial dog will snarl, bark, jump up and possibly scratch at the door. Further-

SMART TIP!

Like children, puppies need structure, rules and praise when they do right, as well as corrections when they make mistakes and a place they can go to feel safe. By showing your puppy what you want, keeping her on a schedule, rewarding her for good behavior and providing a crate or safe room where she can stay when you can't supervise, you will prevent destructive behavior.

more, a territorial dog will show dominant body language — ears straining forward, tail and body held stiff, the fur along his spine raised. An exuberant greeter, on the other hand, will bark, jump, wag his tail, and run around near the door, wiggling, bouncing with delight, ears relaxed and/or back.

Escape artists will also try to rush the door. You know the type. The grass is always greener with the dog down the block. Escape artists lie in hiding, waiting for their chance. The doorbell rings, you open the door, and — *whoosh!* — out rushes your puppy, initiating an exhausting chase through the neighborhood. Usually, your puppy will return in his own sweet time after a romp with the dogs around the block, a snack on the long-dead squirrel carcass in the woods (and a roll in it), and a bath in muddy puddle water. Finally home, he'll shake with satisfaction once inside, covering you in stinky, muddy goo as you tremble with fury, trying very hard not to yell at him because he did make the correct choice to come home, no matter how long he took.

The best method of addressing the door-rushing behavior is to form a positive pattern. Begin by always having your puppy stop and sit/stay or down/stay at the door. He shouldn't cross the threshold until you tell him to heel first. Condition him through repetition. Vary the lengths of the stays and

Cat got your dog's attention? Let your pets play under your supervision, without it getting out of hand. Who knows? Once they establish a social order, they might become good friends.

Mouthing and Chewing

Solve these mouthing-off problems with the following recipes for success.

Mouthing: Mouthing behavior is often seen in young puppies. Puppies mouth objects when they play. Assertive dogs use their mouths to make the point that they are in charge. You should never, at any time, allow your puppy to mouth you. There's no such thing as soft mouthing while playing a game; someone can still be injured. If you allow it, your puppy will pick up the wrong idea about her place in the family pack.

Redirect your puppy when she starts mouthing by showing her a toy and moving it around. Dogs go after movement. The moving toy becomes more interesting than your stationary arm or foot. However, if you're moving an appendage around as you try to dislodge her teeth, you've made the game more interesting.

Another thing you can do is to startle her by saying "ow!" in a high-pitched, yipping tone of voice. As soon as your dog lets go, redirect her to a toy and play with her. The only reason she's mouthing you is to get you into the game. Play the game according to your rules, and you can better control your puppy's behavior.

Chewing: Most puppies will chew anything. They are testing the objects' palatability, as well as learning about their environment. It will be up to you to guide your puppy in the right direction. Make sure your dog has a wide variety of chew toys appropriate for her breed and size.

To maintain your puppy's interest in her toys, rotate their use by briefly "retiring" them so that she thinks she's constantly getting new toys. The "newer" toys maintain her interest for longer periods of time. If your puppy is in the process of teething, offer frozen toys such as ice cubes or washcloths that have been dampened, twisted and placed in the freezer. The cold toys will give her gums relief, thus reducing teething stress.

With plenty of toys around, you can easily redirect your puppy from chewing a table leg to playing with one of her toys. This will require you to constantly observe her activities, but your diligence will pay off in the end, when she knows that your furniture isn't part of her toy box.

the cues given afterward. For example, on one occasion, pass through your doorway and give the heel cue. On another occasion, have your puppy perform a recall back into the house. He has to understand that an open door doesn't always mean that he's going out.

As your dog accomplishes the short stays, aim for longer ones. Also practice walking around him and hiding behind the door or around the outside wall. Distraction proof him by having other people or another dog walk through the doorway.

During the training process, it's a good idea to always keep a 4- to 6-foot leash on your puppy while he's inside. This will allow you to stop his escape by either grabbing or stepping on the leash as he's on his way through the door. Then you can give him his sit/stay or down/stay cue, and you will have the means of making certain he follows through. If you happen to have your clicker and treats with you, use them. If not, as is often the case, just praise and pet him. Always show him how much more rewarding it is to remain inside instead of racing through the door. If your puppy is escaping with the sole purpose of socializing, then you might want to consider getting a second dog. If the grass is greener at home, he'll tend to remain there.

The stay-at-the-door exercise will also help the exuberant greeter. It teaches him that no one will reward him with touch if he

doesn't first control himself. You will need to instruct all people entering your home that they shouldn't touch your puppy until he settles down, so that he isn't rewarded in any fashion for jumping around. After your puppy remains in his stay for at least a minute, you can release him and pet him, provided he remains sitting. As soon as he pops up, stop petting. Don't give in to people who say, "It's OK; he's just a puppy" or, "It's OK; he just wants to say hello." No excuses. This is an annoying behavior that can escalate or hurt someone. Be consistent, and either instruct others in the techniques or don't allow them access to the dog.

The cure for a territorial dog is a little more difficult. There is much you'll need to do to redirect his behavior without extinguishing his effectiveness as a watch dog. First, establish a quiet cue, such as "enough," "quiet" or "shush," since barking is part of his rushing-at-the-door behavior. Reward your puppy profusely when he heeds this cue, even if he heeds it minutes after you issue it. Second, you'll need a means of redirecting and reinforcing. Redirecting can be done with a bell or rattle. Once your puppy is distracted from his barking and is investigating the source of the sound, click and reward.

If your puppy doesn't care about the rattle/ring, you'll have to back up your quiet cue by holding his leash and making him perform a down/stay. It would be far better to have him do a down/stay than a sit because the down is a more submissive posture, and it's more difficult for him to move once in that position. However, if you don't have the means to back up your quiet cue (that is, no collar and leash) you'll need some other means of reinforcing your desires. Try giving a spray of water or citronella, shaking your noise box, or taking hold of your dog and gently pushing down on his nose as you stare into his eyes and say a low-toned "no." It's a good idea to utilize a head halter at this time. Sometimes it's easier to apply pressure on your puppy's nose via a leash and head

If you "make the grass greener" at home, by providing a safe environment for your pup, he will be less likely to rush out the door every time it opens.

halter than to try to hold him still long enough to grab his muzzle. The speed with which you correct the behavior is important. If allowed to continue for even a few minutes, the behavior will be its own reward.

Practice having your puppy come to you every time he hears a knock on the door or the ring of the doorbell. Teach him how to direct himself at these cues. Repetition will condition him.

Once you have your puppy's attention, always reinforce this and reward him. He has to learn that it is far more positive to pay attention and restrain himself than to ignore you and engage in behavioral outbursts. Remember: Make the grass greenest on your side of the fence, and your puppy will come to your way of thinking.

The sit/stay and down/stay cues can prove very useful in keeping escape artists in the house and exuberant greeters off your visitors' laps.

Reality isn't always a fenced yard or a quiet living room. Reality is a walk in the neighborhood; a run in the park; meeting other animals and people; hiking, biking, swimming and more. There are myriad distractions in the real world. A good dog learns how to enjoy this stimulation while remaining responsive to his family. This dog can go anywhere with you and is a perfect addition to any family outing. With distraction proofing and good training, your puppy will become an enjoyable companion for many family activities.

DISTRACTION PROOFING

Distraction proofing is a big part of your puppy's training. Once he can perform his obedience routines reliably indoors and outdoors in a quiet, safely enclosed space, start adding some minor distractions. Leave a few of his toys lying around and ask a friend or family member to walk around, clap their hands, slap their legs, make noise and toss the toys.

Distractions should be introduced in a sequence eventually during all learned cues, as follows:

1. Your puppy must first learn to listen with his toys present. Start by putting your dog in a sit.

2. When your puppy understands that he is supposed to pay attention to you instead of the toys, add a person to the training setting.

3. Have the other person move around the area, then add noises such as whistling or clapping.

4. Next, have the person jog around the area where you are training.

SMART TIP!

Before you begin working with your puppy on a longer leash, make certain that she can perform amid all distractions while on her 6-foot lead. Avoid having to fumble with a handful of leash while trying to distraction-proof your dog.

5. The person should then pick up and drop the toys.

6. With that accomplished, the person should begin throwing the toys around — far from your puppy at first, then closer and closer as your puppy ignores the toys and watches you instead.

Once you've accomplished distraction proofing with toys, it's time for the presence of another dog. This often can be the most difficult distraction (except maybe for the presence of a cat, squirrel or rabbit). The other dog should be one who is already well trained and will not be distracted by your dog. Otherwise, both dogs may be more focused on playing with each other than paying attention to you.

Begin with the second dog at a distance, far enough away so that your puppy takes little notice. Gradually bring the other dog closer and closer. When your puppy begins to look at the other dog, do not bring the other dog any closer. To maintain your dog's attention, you'll need to shape his response to you. When he looks at you, click and reward. When he looks away from you, do something that will regain his attention, such as a sharp turn.

Often, when confronted with a desirable distraction, such as another dog, no amount of treats, toys or coaxing will work to regain your dog's attention. Your dog won't care if you ignore him or take away his

reward. The only thing that might work is to use a head halter to apply pressure on his nose or a collar to deliver a quick reminder that he should pay attention to you. The tool you use depends on your skill level and on your dog. While most dogs can be taught to pay attention and not be distracted by wearing a head halter, many will never adjust to wearing one. In this case, consult a professional dog trainer, who should know what tool to use and can teach you how to effectively use it without causing physical or mental damage.

Once you have that first distance conquered, continue to gradually decrease the distance between the two dogs again. Every time your puppy looks at you, click and reward. When he looks away, apply the head halter to redirect. You should also use your voice, praising when your puppy looks at you and correcting when he looks away. Eventually, all you will need is your voice, but initially you will need to reinforce with a well-timed bridge, reward and use of the training tool.

Distraction proofing can be shaped into place with any and all behaviors. First, your puppy must fully understand each exercise. Then, gradually add the distractions as previously described. In time, your puppy will perform everything you request, regardless of what is going on around him. This takes time, patience and lots of repetition.

As with all training, don't increase the difficulty until you've achieved continuous success at each step. You want to maintain a positive training session with your dog. Be certain that you end on a good note, with your puppy performing well and receiving praise.

TRAVELING

With home distractions accomplished, it's time to venture out and about. Regardless of the type of vehicle you drive, he needs to be — and feel — secure. If you have the space in your vehicle for a travel

crate, use one. If not, use a doggie seat belt; these are seat belts made just for dogs, available for all canine shapes and sizes. Take the time to acclimate your puppy to the crate or seat belt, as well as to the fact that he's in a vehicle. Some dogs suffer from motion sickness or varying degrees of claustrophobia and react poorly to travel, while others love it. If you present traveling in a positive manner and take time to get him used to it, your puppy will be more apt to enjoy traveling.

Here are some tips to acclimate your dog to car travel. If your puppy jumps right into the car, ready to go, you can skip these steps. If not, take your time and gradually teach your dog to accept vehicle travel.

Step 1:
■ Lure your puppy into your vehicle, using high-value treats.

■ Allow him to remain inside; praise and give him treats. You can even offer him a meal in the car. If you are using a crate, pet him while he remains inside. If using a seat belt, rub his chest as he remains in a sit/stay while the belt is on.

This step will teach your puppy that good things happen inside the vehicle. Don't drive anywhere yet. Repeat this exercise every day for about a week so that he can become more comfortable in the car.

Step 2:
◆ Have a family member or a friend pet your puppy and give him treats as you drive around the block or around a parking lot. Drive smoothly. This initial trip should last only 10 to 15 minutes.

◆ Allow your puppy to exit the vehicle in a calm manner, calling him to come and sit in front of you. Combining obedience routines with new experiences helps your dog develop confidence.

◆ The next trip should be a few minutes

Training will strengthen the bond between you and your dog. Take the time to invest in this important activity, and your dog will always be happy to see you.

longer. If you live close to a park, take him there and allow him to play after he gets out of the vehicle. If he gets to go somewhere interesting and fun, he will associate car rides as positive experiences. When car rides end only at the veterinarian's office, it's easy to see how traveling would be a negative experience for your puppy.

◆ When your puppy is comfortable riding without having to receive loads of attention and treats, you can take him for rides without the help of someone offering comfort. Again begin with 10- to 15-minute rides and gradually increase their length.

Once your dog is comfortable with traveling in the car, you can start to increase distances and add more destinations.

TRAINING SUCCESS

A trained dog is a valued member of any family. He's a child who never grows up and never leaves home, a companion, a confidant, and a loyal, loving, intelligent creature who warms your heart and soothes your soul. Take a few minutes each day to train your dog into the perfect family member with whom you will cherish a lifetime of memories and experiences.

ORGANIZATIONS

American Animal Hospital Association
12575 West Bayaud Ave.
Lakewood, CO 80228
303-986-2800
www.healthypet.com

American Dog Owners Association Inc.
P.O. Box 41194
Fredericksburg, VA 22404
888-714-7220
www.adoa.org

American Humane Association
63 Inverness Drive E.
Englewood, CO 80112
800-227-4645, 303-792-9900
www.americanhumane.org

American Kennel Club
8051 Arco Corporate Drive
Suite 100
Raleigh, NC 27617-3390
919-233-9767
www.akc.org

American Kennel Club
Canine Health Foundation
P.O. Box 900061
Raleigh, NC 27675-9061
888-682-9696
www.akcchf.org

American Pet Association
307 W. 200 S.
Suite 2004
Salt Lake City, UT 84101
www.apapets.com

American Society for the Prevention of Cruelty to Animals
424 E. 92nd St.
New York City, NY 10128
212-876-7700
www.aspca.org

American Veterinary Medical Association
1931 North Meacham Road
Suite 100
Schaumburg, IL 60173-4360
800-248-2862
www.avma.org

Association of American Feed Control Officials Inc.
P.O. Box 478
Oxford, IN 47971
765-385-1029
www.aafco.org

Association of Pet Dog Trainers
101 N. Main St.
Suite 610
Greenville, SC 29610
800-738-3647
www.apdt.com

National Association of Professional Pet Sitters
17000 Commerce Parkway
Suite C
Mount Laurel, NJ 08054
856-439-0324,
800-296-7387
www.petsitters.org

SPAY/USA
2261 Broadbridge Ave.
Stratford, CT 06614
203-377-1116
www.spayusa.org

Therapy Dogs Inc.
P.O. Box 20227
Cheyenne, WY 82003
877-843-7364
www.therapydogs.com

United Kennel Club
100 E. Kilgore Road
Kalamazoo, MI 49002-5584
269-343-9020
www.ukcdogs.com

BOOKS

Ask the Vet About Dogs: Easy Answers to Commonly Asked Questions
by Leslie Sinclair
BowTie Press, 2003

ASPCA Complete Guide to Dogs: Everything You Need to Know About Choosing and Caring for Your Pet
by Sheldon L. Gerstenfeld, V.M.D., et al.
Chronicle Books, 1999

Beyond Fetch: Fun, Interactive Activities for You and Your Dog
by D. Caroline Coile, Ph.D.
Howell Book House, 2003

Doggy Desserts
by Cheryl Gianfrancesco
BowTie Press, 2007

Dogs for Kids: Everything You Need to Know About Dogs
by Kristin Mehus-Roe
BowTie Press, 2007

The Original Dog Bible
by Kristin Mehus-Roe
BowTie Press, 2009

Dog Training for Dummies
by Jack Volhard and Wendy Volhard
Wiley Publishing, 2001

Dog Training with a Head Halter
by Miriam Fields-Babineau
Barron's Educational Series, 2000

Dr. Khalsa's Natural Dog:
A Holistic Guide for Healthier Dogs
by Deva Khalsa, D.V.M.
Kennel Club Books, 2009

Marc Morrone's Ask the Dog Keeper
By Marc Morrone
BowTie Press, 2009

Pets Gone Green
By Eve Adamson
BowTie Press, 2009

Simple Solutions® Series:
    Aggression
    Barking
    Chewing
    Clicker Training
    Come, Sit, Stay
    Digging
    Grooming
    Housetraining
    Obedience
    Obesity
    Safety
    Socialization
    Training Your Dog
    Tricks and Games
    Tricks for Treats
BowTie Press, 2002-2010

The ABCs of Positive Training:
A Rewarding Approach for All Owners
by Miriam Fields-Babineau
Kennel Club Books, 2005

What Color Is Your Dog?
Train Your Dog Based on
His Personality "Color"
by Joel Silverman
Kennel Club Books, 2009

WEBSITES

www.animalhealthchannel.com
Animal Health Channel; pet health and behavior information and online health videos

www.clickertraining.com
Karen Pryor Clickertraining; website maintained by a founder of clickertraining

www.dogchannel.com
DOG FANCY magazine online; general dog information

www.dogtrainingbasics.com
Dog Training Basics; training tips from a professional dog behavior consultant and trainer

INDEX

Want More Information about your

Best Friend?

GET **DOGFANCY** EVERY MONTH FOR A SPECIAL LOW PRICE OF ONLY $17.97 FOR A WHOLE YEAR!

Subscribe Today!

DogFancy.com/SmartOwnersGuide

Or call (800) 896-4939 and give code E907DSOG.

PUPPY TRAINING, a Smart Owner's Guide™

part of the Kennel Club Books® Interactive Series™

JOIN Club Pup™ TODAY!

LIBRARY OF CONGRESS CATALOGING-IN-PUBLICATION DATA

McLennan, Bardi.
  Puppy training / Bardi McLennan, Miriam Fields-Babineau.
    p. cm. — (A smart owner's guide)
  Includes bibliographical references and index.
  ISBN 978-1-59378-743-1 (alk. paper)
  1. Puppies—Training. I. Fields-Babineau, Miriam. II. Title.

SF431.M4664 2010
636.7'0887–dc22

                    2010009711